EMPTY THREAT OR SERIOUS DANGER: ASSESSING NORTH KOREA'S RISK TO THE HOMELAND

HEARING

BEFORE THE

SUBCOMMITTEE ON OVERSIGHT AND MANAGEMENT EFFICIENCY

OF THE

COMMITTEE ON HOMELAND SECURITY HOUSE OF REPRESENTATIVES

ONE HUNDRED FIFTEENTH CONGRESS

FIRST SESSION

OCTOBER 12, 2017

Serial No. 115–33

Printed for the use of the Committee on Homeland Security

Available via the World Wide Web: http://www.govinfo.gov

U.S. GOVERNMENT PUBLISHING OFFICE

28–820 PDF   WASHINGTON : 2018

For sale by the Superintendent of Documents, U.S. Government Publishing Office
Internet: bookstore.gpo.gov   Phone: toll free (866) 512–1800; DC area (202) 512–1800
Fax: (202) 512–2104   Mail: Stop IDCC, Washington, DC 20402–0001

COMMITTEE ON HOMELAND SECURITY

MICHAEL T. MCCAUL, Texas, *Chairman*

LAMAR SMITH, Texas
PETER T. KING, New York
MIKE ROGERS, Alabama
JEFF DUNCAN, South Carolina
LOU BARLETTA, Pennsylvania
SCOTT PERRY, Pennsylvania
JOHN KATKO, New York
WILL HURD, Texas
MARTHA MCSALLY, Arizona
JOHN RATCLIFFE, Texas
DANIEL M. DONOVAN, JR., New York
MIKE GALLAGHER, Wisconsin
CLAY HIGGINS, Louisiana
JOHN H. RUTHERFORD, Florida
THOMAS A. GARRETT, JR., Virginia
BRIAN K. FITZPATRICK, Pennsylvania
RON ESTES, Kansas

BENNIE G. THOMPSON, Mississippi
SHEILA JACKSON LEE, Texas
JAMES R. LANGEVIN, Rhode Island
CEDRIC L. RICHMOND, Louisiana
WILLIAM R. KEATING, Massachusetts
DONALD M. PAYNE, JR., New Jersey
FILEMON VELA, Texas
BONNIE WATSON COLEMAN, New Jersey
KATHLEEN M. RICE, New York
J. LUIS CORREA, California
VAL BUTLER DEMINGS, Florida
NANETTE DIAZ BARRAGÁN, California

BRENDAN P. SHIELDS, *Staff Director*
STEVEN S. GIAIER, *Deputy Chief Counsel*
MICHAEL S. TWINCHEK, *Chief Clerk*
HOPE GOINS, *Minority Staff Director*

————

SUBCOMMITTEE ON OVERSIGHT AND MANAGEMENT EFFICIENCY

SCOTT PERRY, Pennsylvania, *Chairman*

JEFF DUNCAN, South Carolina
JOHN RATCLIFFE, Texas
CLAY HIGGINS, Louisiana
RON ESTES, Kansas
MICHAEL T. MCCAUL, Texas *(ex officio)*

J. LUIS CORREA, California
KATHLEEN M. RICE, New York
NANETTE DIAZ BARRAGÁN, California
BENNIE G. THOMPSON, Mississippi *(ex officio)*

RYAN CONSAUL, *Subcommittee Staff Director*
ERICA D. WOODS, *Interim Subcommittee Minority Staff Director*

CONTENTS

Page

EMPTY THREAT OR SERIOUS DANGER: ASSESSING NORTH KOREA'S RISK TO THE HOMELAND

Thursday, October 12, 2017

U.S. HOUSE OF REPRESENTATIVES,
COMMITTEE ON HOMELAND SECURITY,
SUBCOMMITTEE ON OVERSIGHT AND
MANAGEMENT EFFICIENCY,
Washington, DC.

The subcommittee met, pursuant to notice, at 2:02 p.m., in room HVC–210, Capitol Visitor Center, Hon. Scott Perry (Chairman of the subcommittee) presiding.

Present: Representatives Duncan, Higgins, Estes, Perry, Correa, Rice, and Barragán.

Also present: Representative Jackson Lee.

Mr. PERRY. Good afternoon, everybody. The Committee on Homeland Security, Subcommittee on Oversight and Management Efficiency will come to order.

The purpose of this hearing is to examine the risks posed by North Korea to Homeland Security, and recommendations for the Department of Homeland Security to be better prepared to mitigate these risks. The Chair recognizes himself for an opening statement.

It is no secret that Kim Jong-un and his maniacal regime in North Korea have ratcheted up tensions with the United States at an alarming rate. With the knowledge that North Korea conducted over 20 missile tests on over a dozen different occasions between February and September 2017, including tests of intercontinental ballistic missiles, many Americans and our allies around the globe remain on edge. However, Americans may rightly wonder about North Korea's ability to threaten the homeland directly.

Intelligence from the hermit kingdom is oftentimes inconsistent and limited. Despite these intelligence challenges, information that has been gathered is reason enough for alarm. For example, according to media reports, two North Korean shipments to a Syrian government agency responsible for the country's chemical weapons program were intercepted in the past 6 months. While these reports did not detail exactly what the shipments to Syria contained, this is not the first time a North Korean ship has been seized due to carrying suspected missile system components. In 2013, a North Korean ship was intercepted in the Panama Canal with false manifests, and hidden under legitimate cargo parts for fighter jets and rockets.

In addition, according to the Council on Foreign Relations, recent estimates suggest that North Korea's nuclear weapons stockpile comprises 10 to 16 nuclear weapons, and has the potential to grow rapidly by 2020 to potentially 125 weapons. Furthermore, the Center of Nonproliferation Studies estimates North Korea has between 2,500 and 5,000 metric tons of chemical weapons. And as we are all aware with the assassination of Kim Jong-un's half brother with a deadly nerve agent, those weapons have already been put to use.

Whether or not North Korea intends to act on any of its threats to the United States directly, we must also keep in mind that Pyongyang is willing and able to supply weaponry, expertise, or technology to other hostile nation-states and possibly non-nation-state actors that are intent on destroying the United States and the freedoms we stand for.

Former Department of Homeland Security Secretary John Kelly stated in April that the most eminent threat from North Korea is a cyber threat. North Korea's increasingly sophisticated cyber program has the ability to pose a major threat to the United States' interests. For example, Federal prosecutors are investigating North Korea for a possible role in the international banking system, or the SWIFT, hack that resulted in the theft of $81 million from the Central Bank of Bangladesh in 2016. In late 2014, the computer systems of Sony Pictures Entertainment were infiltrated, which was said to have been in retaliation over expressed outrage over the Sony-backed film centered on Kim Jong-un.

With a growing variety of digital threats against the private sector and Federal networks, are we prepared to safeguard our infrastructure against a North Korean-led cyber attack? While a cyber attack from North Korea is a serious risk we face, we cannot discount other possible threats, such as an electromagnetic pulse, or an EMP. An EMP, while some believe as a low probability, has the potential to be a catastrophic event that could result in paralyzing the United States electric grid and other key infrastructure that rely on the electric grid to function.

Disruption to our power grids would be disastrous. According to a 2016 Government Accountability Office, or GAO, report, a major EMP event could result in potential cascading impacts on fuel distribution, transportation system, food and water supplies, and communications and equipment for emergency services.

As North Korea continues its belligerent actions, the United States must be prepared to protect the homeland from an array of threats. The Department of Homeland Security has a vital role in protecting our cyber space and critical infrastructure, and preventing chemical, biological, radiological, and nuclear terrorism.

This hearing will allow us to gain a greater understanding of the multitude, severity, and probability of threats posed by North Korea, and how the Department of Homeland Security can best prepare for and mitigate these risks.

[The statement of Chairman Perry follows:]

STATEMENT OF CHAIRMAN SCOTT PERRY

OCTOBER 12, 2017

It is no secret that Kim Jong-un and his maniacal regime in North Korea have ratcheted up tensions with the United States at an alarming rate. With the knowledge that North Korea conducted over 20 missile tests on over a dozen different occasions between February and September 2017—including tests of intercontinental ballistic missiles, many Americans and our allies around the globe remain on edge. However, Americans may rightly wonder about North Korea's ability to threaten the homeland directly. Intelligence from the "Hermit Kingdom" is oftentimes inconsistent and limited. Despite these intelligence challenges, information that has been gathered is reason enough for alarm.

For example, according to media reports, two North Korean shipments to a Syrian government agency responsible for the country's chemical weapons program were intercepted in the past 6 months. While these reports did not detail exactly what the shipments to Syria contained, this is not the first time a North Korean ship has been seized due to carrying suspected missile-system components. In 2013, a North Korean ship was intercepted in the Panama Canal with false manifests, and hidden under legitimate cargo, parts for fighter jets and rockets.

In addition, according to the Council on Foreign Relations, recent estimates suggest that North Korea's nuclear weapons stockpile comprises 10 to 16 nuclear weapons, and has the potential to grow rapidly by 2020, to potentially 125 weapons. Furthermore, the Center for Nonproliferation Studies estimates North Korea has between 2,500 and 5,000 metric tons of chemical weapons, and as we are all aware with the assassination of Kim Jong-un's half-brother with a deadly nerve agent, those weapons have already been put to use. Whether or not North Korea intends to act on any of its threats to the United States directly, we must also keep in mind that Pyongyang is willing and able to supply weaponry, expertise, or technology to other hostile nation-states, and possibly non nation-state actors that are intent on destroying the United States and the freedoms we stand for.

Former Department of Homeland Security Secretary, John Kelly, stated in April that the most imminent threat from North Korea is a cyber threat. North Korea's increasingly sophisticated cyber program has the ability to pose a major threat to U.S. interests. For example, Federal prosecutors are investigating North Korea for a possible role in the international banking system, SWIFT, hack that resulted in the theft of $81 million from the central bank of Bangladesh in 2016. In late 2014, the computer systems of SONY Pictures Entertainment were infiltrated, which was said to have been in retaliation over expressed outrage over the Sony-backed film centered on Kim Jong-un.

With a growing variety of digital threats against the private sector and Federal networks, are we prepared to safeguard our infrastructure against a North Korean-led cyber attack?

While a cyber attack from North Korea is a serious risk we face, we cannot discount other possible threats, such as an electromagnetic pulse event (EMP). An EMP, while some believe as a low probability, has the potential to be a catastrophic event that could result in paralyzing the U.S. electric grid and other key infrastructures that rely on the electric grid to function. Disruption to our power grids would be disastrous. According to a 2016 Government Accountability Office (GAO) Report, a major EMP event could result in "potential cascading impacts on fuel distribution, transportation systems, food and water supplies, and communications and equipment for emergency services."

As North Korea continues its belligerent actions, the United States must be prepared to protect the homeland from an array of threats. The Department of Homeland Security has a vital role in protecting our cyber space and critical infrastructure and preventing chemical, biological, radiological, and nuclear terrorism. This hearing will allow us to gain a greater understanding of the multitude, severity, and probability of threats posed by North Korea and how the Department of Homeland Security can best prepare for and mitigate these risks.

Mr. PERRY. The Chair now recognizes the Ranking Minority Member of the subcommittee, the gentleman from California, Mr. Correa, for a statement.

Mr. CORREA. Thank you, Chairman Perry. Welcome all our guests here today, the panelists. Thank you, sir, for holding today's hearing on threats of North Korea to our great country. Again, I thank the witnesses for being here today.

I also want to take a moment to send my thoughts and prayers to those affected by the California, southern California wildfires. In my district, many folks very near and dear to me have been evacuated. My staffers and friends have had to be evacuated from their homes, and a couple of camps receiving those evacuated are actually in my district. So our thoughts and prayers are with them as well as others in California.

I also want to thank the first responders for, again, doing the work they are doing right now in and around my district.

Mr. Chairman, while I recognize the seriousness of North Korea and threats it poses to us, I just want to take a moment to acknowledge that we also have to look at those affected by Hurricanes Harvey, Irma, and Maria, and I hope we give them attention as well.

Coming back to North Korea, America's current diplomatic policy must be cautious in engaging this individual, this leadership that appears to be very unpredictable. Reports do confirm that North Korea's accelerating the pace of its missile testing, devoting more of its resources to develop its cyber operations, and threatening to create a multifunctional nuclear bomb.

Recent actions, such as the North Korean-connected hacking group that successfully stole $81 million from banks in Bangladesh and southeast Asia, show that North Korea is getting more daring and much more functional with their cyber operations.

From the witnesses today, I look forward to hearing from you and how this Department of Homeland Security can better protect the vulnerable, critical infrastructure of cyber, cyber threats, and how we can mitigate such threats here in our country.

Further, while the probability of an electromagnetic pulse appears to be at this time unlikely, North Korea has made it clear that it is testing its ability to make a hydrogen bomb capable of such destruction. So my question to you is, is an EMP something that is a threat at this time or very soon?

Speaking on his frustration with President Trump, North Korea's leader stated that Trump "denied the existence of and insulted me and my country in front of the eyes of the world." My question in this, is this anything new or is this what has been going on for the last 20 years?

I am interested in hearing today from the witnesses in this panel, what happens if the unthinkable happens? What would happen the first 10, 20, 30 minutes of an all-out war? A hypothetical scenario, but I think it is one that we need to be apprised of.

With that, Mr. Chair, I thank you. I yield back the balance of my time.

[The statement of Ranking Member Correa follows:]

STATEMENT OF RANKING MEMBER J. LUIS CORREA

OCTOBER 12, 2017

I would like to take a moment to send my thoughts and prayers to those in California, including my home district, affected by devastating wildfires. Thank you to the first responders and local emergency personnel for acting so quickly to evacuate impacted areas to save lives and protect property.

I would also like to take a moment to acknowledge those affected by Hurricanes Harvey, Irma, and Maria. I am frustrated by the slow response by FEMA and the Trump administration, particularly for Puerto Rico. Instead of blaming victims, President Trump should be ensuring his administration gets aid to those without water, food, and electricity and working with stakeholders to help devastated communities recover.

Further, while I recognize the serious National security threat posed by North Korea, I would note that there are pressing matters squarely within this committee's jurisdiction and oversight responsibilities. I hope we can give them the attention they are due.

In regards to North Korea, America's current diplomatic policy is a dangerous game—to engage in a public threat war with the world's most unpredictable bully. According to experts, President Trump's unabashedly undiplomatic rhetoric—threatening to destroy North Korea—has created an impression that it is actually the United States, instead of North Korea, that is motivated by aggression.

Clearly, North Korea is stepping up the pace of its missile testing, devoting more resources to further develop its cyber operations, and threatening the creation of a multi-functional nuclear bomb with destructive power.

Recent actions—such as a North Korea-connected hacking group successfully stealing $81 million from banks in Bangladesh and Southeast Asia—show that North Korea is getting more daring with its cyber operations.

I look forward to hearing from the witnesses today how the Department of Homeland Security can better protect vulnerable critical infrastructure in response to cyber threats and provide assistance in mitigation efforts. Further, while the probability of an EMP attack is unlikely, North Korea has made it clear it is testing its ability to make a hydrogen bomb capable of such destruction.

Speaking on his frustrations with Trump, North Korea's leader, Kim Jong-Un, stated that Trump "denied the existence of and insulted me and my country in front of the eyes of the world." President Trump's own words aid North Korea's propaganda and create pressure for North Korea to respond with its own provocation.

I also look forward to today's witnesses addressing how this administration has escalated the situation with North Korea and exacerbated an already-serious foreign policy matter.

Mr. PERRY. The Chair thanks the gentleman, and would also like to join you in echoing my concerns for those affected in and around your district, and of course in California, the wildfires, and the first responders, as well as the victims of the recent hurricanes here in the continental United States and our citizens in Puerto Rico and the Caribbean.

With that, other Members of the subcommittee are reminded that opening statements may be submitted for the record.

[The statement of Ranking Member Thompson follows:]

STATEMENT OF RANKING MEMBER BENNIE G. THOMPSON

OCTOBER 12, 2017

Undoubtedly, the threat posed by North Korea is one of the most complex challenges to our National security. Daily, we hear of North Korea's targeting our Nation—including our way of life. These threats, if carried out, could cause unprecedented devastation to our Nation.

Under the Kim Jong-un regime, North Korea has executed 98 ballistic missile tests and 6 underground nuclear tests overall. This year alone, North Korea has fired 22 missiles during 15 tests, including an intercontinental ballistic missile (ICBM)—a missile that is reported to reach anywhere in the world—launched on July 4, 2017.

Given the relationship between the United States and North Korea, it can be concluded that the purpose of the tests is producing missiles capable of reaching this country. North Korea's cyber capabilities also raise serious concerns, as the effects of cyber warfare can be crippling.

Along with Russia, U.S. intelligence officials have long considered North Korea among the world's most dangerous cyber actors in terms of their ability to inflict damage via computer networks. The intelligence community has warned that North Korea has plans to execute a large-scale cyber attack on our critical infrastructure.

Furthermore, according to a recent and alarming CNN article, a Russian telecommunications firm is now providing North Korea a new internet connection, thus potentially augmenting North Korea's cyber attacking capabilities while deepening its ties to the Nation responsible for hacking the 2016 U.S. election.

Today, I see that there is an effort in this body to place a serious focus on this threat. That sentiment is not shared down the street at 1600 Pennsylvania Avenue. Unfortunately, President Trump seemingly is uninterested in handling this threat in a diplomatic fashion.

Instead, the President engages in a public "war of words" with North Korean leader Kim Jong-un, escalating tensions at a time when the need for appropriate sanctions and strategic diplomacy could not be greater. What is also appalling is the President's focus on disparaging the Nation's top diplomat and challenging his IQ.

Instead, the President should devote his attention to the North Korean threat rather than tweeting and hurling insults all for the sake of attention.

I look forward to having a productive discussion on the threats posed by North Korea to the United States and the steps the Department of Homeland Security can take to mitigate those threats.

Mr. PERRY. We are pleased to have a distinguished panel of witnesses before us today. The witnesses' entire written statements will appear in the record. The Chair will introduce the witness first and then recognize each of you for your testimony.

All right. Mr. Frank Cilluffo—is that correct, sir?

Mr. CILLUFFO. That is correct.

Mr. PERRY. All right—is an associate vice president at the George Washington University and director of its Center for Cyber and Homeland Security. He previously served in numerous homeland security positions in the White House and Homeland Security Advisory Council. Welcome, sir.

Mr. Anthony Ruggiero—is that correct or close enough?

Mr. RUGGIERO. Close enough.

Mr. PERRY. OK—is a senior fellow with the Foundation of Defense of Democracies. He served in the Treasury Department as director of the Office of Global Affairs and the Office of Terrorist Financing and Financial Crimes, and spent 13 years in various positions in the State Department. Welcome, sir.

Mr. Patrick Terrell is a senior research fellow at the Center for the Study of WMD, Weapons of Mass Destruction, at the National Defense University. He served in the U.S. Army Chemical Corps for 27 years and was the WMD military adviser and deputy director for chemical, biological, radiological, and nuclear defense policy in the Office of the Deputy Assistant Secretary of Defense for Countering WMD. Sir, thank you for your service and welcome.

Mr. Jeff Greene is a senior director of global government affairs and policy at Symantec, where he leads a team focused on cybersecurity, data integrity, and privacy issues. Prior to joining Symantec, he served in staff positions on the Senate Homeland Security and Governmental Affairs and House Homeland Security Committees and as an attorney with a Washington, DC law firm. Welcome, sir.

Dr. Peter Vincent Pry is a Nationally-recognized expert on electromagnetic pulse, or EMP. Dr. Pry was most recently chief of staff of the EMP Commission, and has served on the staffs of various Congressional commissions related to National security, as well as the House Armed Services Committee, and was an intelligence officer with the Central Intelligence Agency. Welcome, sir.

Thank you all for being here today.

The Chair recognizes now Mr. Cilluffo for an opening statement. Sir.

STATEMENT OF FRANK J. CILLUFFO, DIRECTOR, CENTER FOR CYBER AND HOMELAND SECURITY, THE GEORGE WASHINGTON UNIVERSITY

Mr. CILLUFFO. Chairman Perry, Ranking Member Correa, and distinguished Members of the subcommittee, thank you for the opportunity to testify before you today on such a critical set of issues.

North Korea poses an increasingly complex and multidimensional threat to the U.S. homeland. The many facets of the challenge include, obviously, the nuclear threat, the missile threat, and the proliferation threat. My own remarks will focus on the cyber threat.

As regards to the cyber aspect, it should be flagged up front that it is not one-dimensional. To the contrary, it may manifest itself in at least three ways: As a stand-alone cyber threat; as a component in conjunction with a broader campaign, i.e., military or kinetic means; or as an indicator of an attack or campaign that is yet to come, the cyber equivalent of intelligence preparation of the battlefield or the mapping of our critical infrastructures.

At a conference we co-hosted with the Central Intelligence Agency just last week, a senior CIA official described North Korea as between bookends: The fear of Chinese abandonment on the one hand and the fear of U.S. strike on the other. The official stated further that North Korea exists to oppose the United States, and that Kim Jong-un defines winning as staying in the game. It is against this background, the overriding survival of the Kim regime and the Songun or military-first policy, that the North Korean cyber threat must be considered and evaluated.

In terms of the bottom-line up-front, the cyber threat is already here. It is persistent, on-going, and comes in various guises and forms. The battlefield today includes the traditional air, land, sea, space, but increasingly cyber space, which is simultaneously its own domain and transcends all the other domains.

The question is if and when the North Korean cyber activity escalates, moving higher up the chain of conflict, going beyond traditional computer network exploit and cyber crime to bigger and more destructive attacks. If so, what are the primary targets? How can we thwart the attacks or minimize the impact through contingency planning and building resilience into our networks and systems?

At the high end of the threat spectrum are nation-states whose military and intelligence services are integrating computer network attack and computer network exploit into their warfighting strategy and doctrine.

North Korea is one of a small handful of countries that top the list from a U.S. National security perspective. While many of the details of their actual cyber warfare capabilities are shrouded in secrecy, we do know that North Korea has invested heavily in building out their cyber capabilities. A 2015 report by the South Korean defense ministry estimates that the North Korean cyber army employs an elite squad of 6,000 hackers. This number has likely increased, and it's worth noting that many of these hackers operate outside of Pyongyang, in northeast China and Southeast Asia. While not up yet up to par with the likes of say, Russia or China, what North Korea may lack in capability, it unfortunately more than makes up for with intent.

North Korea has engaged in both extensive espionage as well as disruptive and destructive activities or CNA. They operate without compunction. Recent reports of pilfering of Classified information from the South Korean military and the targeting of U.S. energy companies and other industrial control systems here is troubling and reflective of their persistent espionage. The attack on Sony is just one example of a destructive activity. There are sadly many, many more in South Korea.

But perhaps what differentiates North Korea from other cyber actors is that they have turned to cyber crime to raise revenue, including funding their nuclear aspirations, especially given recent sanctions that are levied upon them. They have been pegged as the likely culprit, as both you, Mr. Chairman, and the Ranking Member have highlighted, behind a string of cyber bank robberies as far as Poland, but also the SWIFT hack on the Central Bank of Bangladesh, hacks against bitcoin and other cryptocurrency exchanges, and the WannaCry ransomware attack, which impacted 150 countries.

If past is prologue, we ought to be prepared for a further spike in North Korean cyber crime. While the cyber twists may be relatively new, such behavior is not. North Korea has long turned to criminal activity, such as counterfeiting, currency, cigarettes, pharmaceuticals, to fill its coffers. Whereas traditionally forces of crime seek to penetrate the state, in the case of North Korea, the opposite is true, with the country often using diplomatic cover to pursue illegal activities. In essence, they are using national collection means, using all source intelligence for criminal gain or more aptly to be compared to as a state sponsor of cyber crime.

One word on what we do about this. Bottom line, we need to train more and better, we need to exercise. I think contingency plans are really important, make the big mistakes on the practice field, not when it is game day. DHS has done some good work in terms of sharing of information intelligence, such as HIDDEN COBRA, where they provided TTPs and indicators of North Korean activity. This is so vital because that is going to be the warning. That is going to be the indicator that something bigger may be afoot.

In terms of the broader threat picture, other potential scenarios like EMP, that will require a much broader response, and it will need to include partners like DOD, as DHS and the utilities would likely be overwhelmed in such a scenario. I hope there is more time to get into that during the Q&A.

Thank you, Mr. Chairman.

[The prepared statement of Mr. Cilluffo follows:]

PREPARED STATEMENT OF FRANK J. CILLUFFO

OCTOBER 12, 2017

Chairman Perry, Ranking Member Correa, and distinguished Members of the subcommittee, thank you for the opportunity to testify before you today on this subject of National importance. North Korea poses an increasingly complex and multidimensional threat to the U.S. homeland. The many facets of the challenge include the nuclear threat, the missile threat, and the proliferation threat—which encompasses North Korea's role in the global arms trade of conventional and non-conventional weapons. Other experts testifying before you today will focus on these and other aspects of the problem. My own remarks will focus on the cyber threat, though I will also touch on the issue of electromagnetic pulse (EMP). As regards the cyber aspect, it should be flagged upfront that it is not unidimensional. To the contrary, it may manifest in at least three ways: As a stand-alone cyber threat; as a cyber component of a broader campaign that makes use of other means (e.g., military); or as an indicator of an attack or campaign that is yet to come (cyber intelligence preparation (IPB) of the battlefield or mapping of critical infrastructure). After assessing the threat, I will turn to the role that DHS can and should play in countering that threat.

THE CYBER THREAT THAT NORTH KOREA POSES TO THE U.S. HOMELAND

At the Central Intelligence Agency (CIA)'s fourth annual public conference on the Ethos and Profession of Intelligence (co-hosted by the George Washington University Center for Cyber & Homeland Security), a senior CIA official described North Korea as between "bookends"—the fear of Chinese abandonment on the one hand, and the fear of a U.S. strike on the other. The official stated further that North Korea "exists to oppose the United States," and that Kim Jong-un "defines winning as staying in the game."[1] It is against this background, the overriding survival of the Kim regime and the "Songun" or military first policy, that the North Korean cyber threat must be considered and evaluated.

In prepared testimony before the full committee[2] and one of your counterpart subcommittees,[3] I have set out in some detail the nature of the cyber threat that North Korea poses to the U.S. homeland. Today I will build further upon that baseline. At the high end of the cyber threat spectrum are nation-states whose military and intelligence services are both determined and sophisticated in the cyber domain and are integrating computer network attack (CNA) and computer network exploit (CNE) into their warfighting strategy and doctrine—North Korea is one of a small handful of countries that top that list from a U.S. National security perspective. While many of the details about North Korea's cyber warfare capabilities are shrouded in secrecy (the same is true of their military capabilities writ large), we do know that North Korea has invested heavily in building cyber capabilities. A 2015 report by the South Korean Defense Ministry estimates that the North Korean "cyber army" employs an elite squad of 6,000 hackers,[4] many of whom operate abroad in northeast China and throughout South East Asia. And, what North Korea may lack in capability, it makes up for with intent.

North Korea has engaged in both disruptive and destructive activity in the cyber domain—meaning both computer network exploitation (CNE) and computer network attack (CNA; as distinct from espionage). North Korea operates without compunction, targeting U.S. companies; the most notorious case being the attack on Sony Pictures Entertainment. North Korea is just as aggressive within its region: In 2017, there has been a major increase in North Korean cyber attacks (attempted and successful) targeting South Korean companies and government.[5] Senior Japanese cybersecurity officials confirmed this in recent meetings, and expressed significant concern about the increase in volume and the level of boldness of North Korean cyber activity. Recent news articles revealing alleged U.S. cyber activities aimed at stymieing North Korea's ballistic missile program will likely serve to increase the likelihood of additional North Korean cyber attacks.

In order to raise revenue—and under particular pressure from sanctions imposed recently by the international community (including key trading partner China), following North Korean nuclear and missile testing—North Korea has turned to cyber crime, and is the prime suspect in a string of bank heists throughout Asia (SWIFT hack), as well as reportedly targeting "bitcoin and other virtual currencies" for theft

---

[1] *https://www.youtube.com/watch?v=a-N__NqVe__uc&list=PL-bQ6__vfcE05kAK-AX3uGxjLk-0bVDhE3O&index=2.*

[2] *https://cchs.gwu.edu/sites/cchs.gwu.edu/files/Cilluffo%20Testimony%20for%20HHSC%203-22-2017.pdf.*

[3] *https://cchs.gwu.edu/sites/cchs.gwu.edu/files/downloads/HHSC__Testimony__Feb%2025-2016__Final.pdf.*

[4] Martin Anderson, "North Korea's Internet Tundra Breeds Specialised 'Cyber Forces' Numbering 6,000," *The Stack*, January 7, 2015. *https://thestack.com/security/2015/01/07/north-koreas-internet-tundra-breeds-specialised-cyber-forces-numbering-6000.*

[5] Charlie Campbell, "The World Can Expect More Cybercrime from North Korea Now that China has Banned its Coal," *Time*, February 19, 2017. *http://time.com/4676204/north-korea-cyber-crime-hacking-china-coal/.*

(FireEye report).[6] It has also been reported that the country is "widely believed to be behind the WannaCry [ransomware] cyber attack which spread to more than 300,000 computers across 150 countries."

STATE SPONSOR OF CYBER CRIME

If past is prologue, we ought to be prepared for a further spike in North Korean State-sponsored and/or State-supported cyber crime. The former head of the United Kingdom's Government Communications Headquarters (GCHQ) reinforced this point the other day, stating bluntly, "They're after our money."[7] While the cyber twist may be relatively new, such behavior is not: North Korea has long turned to criminal activity, such as counterfeiting (of currency including so-called super-notes, pharmaceuticals, and cigarettes), to fill its coffers. In this way, the regime engages criminal proxies and their cyber prowess to help achieve the ends that will perpetuate the regime's survival. This convergence of nation-state and criminal forces heightens the dangers posed by both. Whereas, traditionally, it has been the forces of crime that seek to penetrate the state; in the case of North Korea, the opposite is true, with the country often using diplomatic cover to pursue illegal activities.

North Korea's cyber strategy and tactics must be understood in broader context, as part and parcel of other geopolitical tools and goals (military, political, economic). The country's cyber capabilities are just one weapon in their arsenal, to be used in conjunction with other elements and for the purpose of achieving a wide range of goals and objectives. When assessed and appreciated in this way, North Korea's cyber activity may portend a broader campaign (including military operations), and thereby serve as an indicator or early warning of the intent to strike in other domains. And, cyber crime is undoubtedly helping fund North Korea's nuclear and missile programs. At the same time, from a cyber standpoint, North Korea is less vulnerable (relative to the countries it targets) to retaliation in-kind, since North Korea is not "wired" like most other nation-states. To the extent that the country is connected to the internet—for military and intelligence purposes, for example— it appears that efforts have been made to protect and maintain that cyber capability and resilience, by diversifying connectivity: Just days ago, it was reported that a Russian firm will provide North Korea with a second internet connection, thereby decreasing reliance on the previously single connection that a Chinese firm had provided; and expanding North Korea's cyber attack capability.[8] There has also been chatter about Russian criminal support of North Korea's cyber activities.

A further risk for the United States is electromagnetic pulse (EMP), which includes the threat posed by directed energy weapons. As defined by the Department of Energy, EMPs "are intense pulses of electromagnetic energy resulting from solar-caused effects or man-made nuclear and pulse-power devices."[9] Nuclear EMP in particular—generated by detonating a nuclear device at a high altitude—would have catastrophic effects for the electricity, communications, transportation, fuel, and water sectors (including others). EMP is a threat that the United States must address from both a strategic and operational perspective. In connection with North Korea, it may be tempting to think in binary terms; but we do so at our peril, for cyber tools/attacks, EMPs, missiles, kinetic actions, and so on, are not "either/or" propositions. To the contrary—and, especially, if North Korea does not have the requisite launch capacity for its missiles (be they nuclear-tipped or conventional)—the country may turn to some combination of the foregoing (i.e., cyber plus . . .). Significantly, just last month North Korea publicly stated, for the first time, that they have developed a hydrogen bomb that can be detonated at high altitudes thereby signaling "interest and ability in an EMP attack."[10] While the probability of first use may currently be relatively low, the potential consequences and impact could

---

[6] Luke McNamara, "Why is North Korea So Interested in Bitcoin?" (September 11, 2017), *https://www.fireeye.com/blog/threat-research/2017/09/north-korea-interested-in-bitcoin.html.* See also Ryan Browne, "North Korea appears to be trying to get around sanctions by using hackers to steal bitcoin," (September 12, 2017), *https://www.cnbc.com/2017/09/12/north-korea-hackers-trying-to-steal-bitcoin-evade-sanctions.html.*

[7] Harvey Gavin, "Hacking warning: Kim Jong-Un's henchmen to step up cyber attacks and target city of London," *Express* (October 1, 2017), *http://www.express.co.uk/news/uk/861007/north-korea-hackers-target-uk-banks.*

[8] Reuters Staff, "Russian firm provides new internet connection to North Korea," *Reuters* (Oct. 2, 2017), *http://www.reuters.com/article/us-nkorea-internet/russian-firm-provides-new-internet-connection-to-north-korea-idUSKCN1C70D2?il=0.*

[9] *https://energy.gov/sites/prod/files/2017/01/f34/DOE%20EMP%20Resilience%20Action%-20Plan%20January%202017.pdf* (at page 1).

[10] Anthony Furey, "North Korea openly threatens EMP attack for the first time, changing the game," *Toronto Sun* (September 3, 2017), *http://m.torontosun.com/2017/09/03/north-korea-openly-threatens-emp-attack-for-the-first-time-changing-the-game.*

be catastrophic and, therefore, the possibility must be taken seriously and treated accordingly.

The chart on the following page captures, at a glance, the multidimensional nature of the North Korean cyber threat; and contextualizes it with selected examples.

NORTH KOREA—CYBER THREAT ACTOR

Strategy	Discriptor	Example
Computer Network Attack (CNA).	Disruptive or destructive in nature, cyber-specific/exclusive or in combination with kinetic military operations.	Hack of SONY Pictures Entertainment Inc.
Computer Network Exploitation (CNE).	Espionage (military, economic, and diplomatic), cyber IPB of critical infrastructure can provide important indicators & warning of a broader campaign and attack plans (order of battle).	Persistent, on-going, across a range of sectors and targets
Cyber crime	Theft, ransomware, etc. ...	SWIFT hack, bank and bitcoin theft, Wanna Cry ransomware

THE ROLE OF THE DEPARTMENT OF HOMELAND SECURITY

Preparing for cyber threats from state actors such as North Korea requires a multidimensional response. Accordingly, all elements of statecraft—diplomatic, economic, law enforcement, intelligence, military, emergency preparedness, and so on—should be considered and integrated, as appropriate (including in contingency plans). Whatever the Department of Homeland Security (DHS) does, it must be undertaken with the preparatory efforts of its various partners in mind—including, in particular, the Department of Defense and the private sector. Actions to protect and enhance the resilience of critical infrastructure, moreover, should be undertaken in a manner that recognizes, addresses, and integrates the full spectrum of threats, from cyber to EMP and beyond. There is a need to begin planning and exercising in earnest for various scenarios including EMP—which would have impact beyond DHS and U.S. utilities, given the importance of the electric grid and its interdependencies with all other "lifeline" critical infrastructures.

Policy and programs must not only cohere at the strategic and operational levels within DHS, within the interagency, and across the public/private sector (to ensure that public and private-sector efforts and initiatives are pulling in the same direction). Policy and programs must also complement and leverage those of our international allies and partners, in order to be maximally effective. Others, beyond the United States, could and should do more to contain and crack down on North Korea. The United States is already working with South Korea and Japan, for example; but, geopolitical complexities must be navigated skillfully in order to further pull in other key actors constructively, so as to better deal with the challenges at hand. Keep in mind, for instance, that as pressure increases on China to pull back from North Korea, Russia is stepping into the breach as backstop for Kim Jong-un's regime.

The Department of Homeland Security (DHS) must strategically plan, resource, and prepare for the cyber threat posed by North Korea, and it must do so in the context of the broader threat posed by that country, and as part of the Department's mission writ large, which includes but is not limited to the ".gov" environment. DHS must also do all of this at a time when resources are limited and threats are expanding. The challenge, therefore, is to develop and implement programs that are not only effective but efficient. The Quadrennial Homeland Security Review (QHSR) is one instrument that helps to align strategy imperatives with spending parameters, so that both programming and underwriting are undertaken wisely. However, in the present ecosystem where risks are intensifying, it bears asking (immediately) if the current status of DHS programs and plans is sufficient—or whether there are things that the Department can and should do differently.

The National Protection and Programs Directorate (NPPD) of DHS provides a range of valuable services to support and protect entities directly within its remit (Federal civilian networks) and partners with whom the Department collaborates (State, local, Tribal, and territorial governments, and the private sector). These services range from vulnerability scanning and mitigation guidance, to information sharing and malware analysis, to technical assistance and intrusion-/incident-specific "hunt" teams. Importantly, efforts are underway to "streamline and elevate" the NPPD's cybersecurity and critical infrastructure mission. These activities, together with the multidisciplinary experience and expertise of the Department as a whole (e.g., in law enforcement, risk mitigation, and emergency management, to name a few), allow DHS to help further National resilience, and deter threat actors.[11]

The Department's work on "Hidden Cobra" is a case in point. This attack effort by North Korean government actors targeted U.S. businesses (including critical infrastructure sectors, financial and aerospace companies) using malware and botnet attacks.[12] Working together with the Federal Bureau of Investigation (FBI), DHS provided critical infrastructure owners and operators (85 percent are in the private sector) with crucial situational awareness in the form an alert, attribution, and malware analysis.[13] In its outreach to stakeholders, DHS specified the vulnerabilities that the North Korean perpetrators were using, as well as signatures that could be used for/integrated into response strategies. Importantly, these types of network-defense activities can be very effective in countering North Korea in particular, which has a massive botnet infrastructure. From the standpoint of industry, furthermore, the sort of granular and timely information that DHS provided—including the identity of the attacker and the tactics, techniques, and procedures (TTPs) used—was valuable, as it allowed alerted entities to inoculate themselves against certain vulnerabilities (or, at least, to mitigate the consequences of breach). In addition to identifying TTPs, DHS, and FBI in conjunction with the intelligence community could also provide indications & warning (I&W) of potential North Korean target lists/selection and potential order of battle.

Hidden Cobra is thus illustrative of the interagency process working as it should, with DHS partnering with the Federal community for information exchange, in order for DHS to provide real added value to its stakeholders. The case also ties together the information-sharing component with deterrence, in that the DHS alert and subsequent prevention/mitigation activity on the part of targeted businesses (and the Government) demonstrates to the attacker that the United States is both ready and able to take anticipatory (defensive) action against adversaries or, if need be, to rebound and show resilience post-attack. This evidence of "a virtuous cycle" is what DHS can and should build upon, so as to generate additional positive momentum that in turn will help further fuel its own success. Interagency partners like the Cyber Threat Intelligence Integration Center (CTIIC) have already proven to be willing and capable partners in upping the U.S. game against cyber adversaries: As events unfold, CTIIC brings together information from across the Federal cyber community to form a shared picture of the U.S. Government's information (both Classified and Unclassified), gaps, and actions to inform decision makers who have a role in the response. But still, we need to do more, and we need to do better. In this respect, we should strive for the DHS equivalent to military planning and execution, where all relevant players have a seat at the table pre-incident and where all concerned are well-positioned to thwart attacks and attackers when an incident is underway.

CONCLUSION

Thank you again for this opportunity to testify on this important topic.[14] I look forward to trying to answer any questions that you may have.

Mr. PERRY. The Chair thanks the gentleman.

---

[11] For additional details, see the written testimony of Acting Secretary of Homeland Security Elaine C. Duke, tendered to the Senate Committee on Homeland Security and Governmental Affairs (September 27, 2017), *https://www.hsgac.senate.gov/hearings/09/18/2017/threats-to-the-homeland* (see especially pages 9–11).

[12] Tom Spring "DHS, FBI warn of North Korea 'Hidden Cobra' strikes against US assets," *Threatpost* (June 14, 2017), *https://threatpost.com/dhs-fbi-warn-of-north-korea-hidden-cobra-strikes-against-us-assets/126263/*.

[13] US–CERT Alert (TA 17–164A), "HIDDEN COBRA—North Korea's DDoS Botnet Infrastructure" (June 13, 2017), *https://www.us-cert.gov/ncas/alerts/TA17-164A*.

[14] I would like to thank the Center's Associate Director Sharon Cardash for her help in drafting my prepared testimony.

The Chair now recognizes Mr. Ruggiero—Ruggiero for an opening statement. I threw an I in there. I don't know where it came from, but I threw it in.

STATEMENT OF ANTHONY RUGGIERO, SENIOR FELLOW, FOUNDATION FOR DEFENSE OF DEMOCRACIES

Mr. RUGGIERO. Chairman Perry, Ranking Member Correa, and distinguished Members of the subcommittee, thank you for the opportunity to address you today on this important issue.

North Korea's nuclear weapons and missile programs are expanding after a decade of failed American policies, and now pose a direct threat to the U.S. homeland. Pyongyang has threatened our close allies South Korea and Japan, as well as the U.S. troops stationed for decades on allied territory.

The progress of North Korea's program should not be surprising since Pyongyang conducted its first nuclear test 11 years ago. Its long-range missile program has lasted for more than 20 years. Pyongyang twice tested an intercontinental ballistic missile in July that could target Los Angeles, Denver, and Chicago, and possibly Boston and New York. The Kim regime tested a massive thermonuclear weapon designed to obliterate cities and could be delivered by Pyongyang's long-range missiles.

These developments are more concerning when we consider that Pyongyang has a proclivity for selling weapons to anyone who will pay for them. It has sold items related to nuclear weapons, chemical weapons, and ballistic missiles. Among North Korea's most troubling relationships are those with Iran and Syria. The threat we face is acute and growing. After years of strategic patience, the time has come for a policy of maximum pressure that actually stands a chance of restraining the North Korean threat without resorting to war.

The Trump administration is pursuing Iran-style sanctions to force North Korea to denuclearize. Absent that result, protect the United States and its allies from Pyongyang's activities. Both critics and supporters of the 2015 nuclear deal agree that sanctions were the main driver that brought Iran to the negotiating table. Modeled on the successful Iran sanctions program, the Trump administration's efforts clarify the choice we are asking other countries to make: Do business with North Korea or do business with the United States. It cannot be both.

This approach includes diplomatic efforts to convince other countries to cut ties with North Korea, reinforced by the threat of losing access to the U.S. financial system. The *Wall Street Journal* reported that a year-long effort by the State Department resulted in over 20 countries cutting off diplomatic or commercial relationships with North Korea.

In prior testimonies, I detailed flaws in the current sanctions regime, including a failure to prioritize the North Korea sanctions program and the need to focus on Pyongyang's overseas business network, as well as non-North Koreans facilitating sanctions of Asia.

North Korea's shipping network plays a crucial role in supporting this evasion, including the prohibited transfer of commodities. The Countering America's Adversaries Through Sanctions Act contains several provisions for the Department of Homeland Security that require it to highlight the role of North Korean vessels in illicit transfers and the role of third-party countries facilitating these transfers.

The Department must publish a list of North Korean vessels. Treasury's Office of the Foreign Assets Control currently lists only 40 vessels as blocked property of North Korean designated persons, but our research indicates that more than 140 could be linked to North Korea.

The Department of Homeland Security and other elements of the U.S. Government should focus on the activities of North Korean linked vessels, including increasing the number of entities and individuals sanctioned in the North Korea shipping sector, compiling a complete list of vessels linked to North Korea, and naming ports in China and Russia that facilitate North Korea sanctions of Asia. The urgency of the threat should call for the Department to take these actions before the 180-day grace period granted by the sanctions law is elapsed.

North Korea's nuclear weapons and missile programs are a threat to the U.S. homeland and our allies. There are two basic policy options for the United States. One accepts this dangerous situation as reality under the false premise that North Korea's provocations can be contained or deterred. The other path was successful in bringing Iran to the negotiating table with crushing sanctions that could force the Kim regime to realize the futility of continuing its nuclear weapons and missile programs.

The only peaceful way to protect the U.S. homeland is to ensure Kim Jong-un feels the full weight of sanctions implemented by the United States and our allies.

Thank you again for inviting me, and I look forward to your questions.

[The prepared statement of Mr. Ruggiero follows:]

PREPARED STATEMENT OF ANTHONY RUGGIERO

OCTOBER 12, 2017

Chairman Perry, Ranking Member Correa, and distinguished Members of this subcommittee, thank you for the opportunity to address you today on this important issue.

My testimony will begin with a review of North Korea's nuclear- and missile-related proliferation activities, followed by a discussion of how Iran-style sanctions can sharply increase the amount of pressure on Pyongyang. My testimony will conclude with recommendations for how the Department of Homeland Security (DHS) should implement its mandate to monitor North Korean vessels in order to maximize the impact of sanctions.

North Korea's nuclear weapons and missile programs are expanding after a decade of failed American policies and now pose a direct threat to the U.S. homeland. Pyongyang has threatened our close allies, South Korea and Japan, as well as the U.S. troops stationed for decades on allied territory. The progress of North Korea's programs should not be surprising since Pyongyang conducted its first nuclear test 11 years ago; its weaponization program likely started before then. Its long-range missile program has lasted for more than 20 years and is beginning to show success.

Pyongyang twice tested an intercontinental ballistic missile (ICBM) in July. Both tests were launched in a lofted trajectory to avoid overflying Japan. But technical analysis of the second test on July 28 suggests that North Korean ICBMs could target Los Angeles, Denver, Chicago, and possibly Boston and New York.[1] While an

---

[1] David Wright, "North Korean ICBM Appears Able to Reach Major US Cities," Union of Concerned Scientists, July 28, 2017. (*http://allthingsnuclear.org/dwright/new-north-korean-icbm*)

ICBM may reach that distance, questions remain about the survivability of Pyongyang's missiles during their reentry into Earth's atmosphere, since the effectiveness of the heat shields protecting their warheads is unknown.[2] However, it is important not to underestimate North Korea's ability to overcome these challenges, since Pyongyang's progress on the ICBM program has outpaced the intelligence community's development time lines by 2 years.[3]

Kim Jong-un's regime followed its successful ICBM launches in July with a massive thermonuclear weapon test on September 3. As part of that test, North Korea likely succeeded in detonating a nuclear weapon designed to obliterate cities, which could be delivered by its long-range missiles.[4] The threat we face is acute and growing. After years of passivity justified by the mantra of "strategic patience," the time has come for a policy of "maximum pressure" that actually stands a chance of restraining the threat without resorting to war.

PROLIFERATION CONCERNS [5]

The advances in North Korea's weapons programs are more concerning when we consider that Pyongyang has a proclivity for selling weapons to anyone who will pay for them. It has sold items related to nuclear weapons, chemical weapons, and ballistic missiles. Among North Korea's most troubling relationships are those with Iran and Syria.

Pyongyang and Tehran have a long-standing partnership on missile development, including the transfer of ballistic missiles. The relationship was serious enough for the Obama administration to sanction Iran just a day after implementation of the 2015 nuclear deal began. The Treasury Department reported at the time that Iranian technicians traveled to North Korea to work on rocket boosters and senior officials conducted contract negotiations in Pyongyang.[6]

North Korea and Iran would both stand to gain by extending their cooperation from ballistic missiles to nuclear activities. Pyongyang's nuclear weapons testing has produced useful information that scientists in Iran would be very interested in. There have also been unconfirmed reports of Iranian nuclear scientists at North Korea's nuclear tests.[7] It is unclear how far along Pyongyang's uranium enrichment program is, but Iran can conduct advanced centrifuge research under the 2015 nuclear deal, whose results could be attractive to North Korea.[8] As sanctions on Kim's regime start to bite, it could turn to Iran for hard currency in exchange for nuclear technology and knowledge.

Supporters of the Iran nuclear deal are likely to dismiss these concerns out-of-hand, saying there is no evidence of Iran-North Korea nuclear cooperation, but proliferation is hard to detect. One example is North Korea's construction of a nuclear reactor in Syria, located in an area that would later be controlled by the Islamic State. The reactor was built with North Korean assistance and had "striking similarities" to Pyongyang's plutonium production reactor at Yongbyon.[9]

---

[2] David Wright, "Reentry Heating from North Korea's July 4 Missile Test," Union of Concerned Scientists, July 7, 2017. (*http://allthingsnuclear.org/dwright/july-4-reentry-heating*)

[3] Ellen Nakashima, Anna Fifield, and Joby Warrick, "North Korea could cross ICBM threshold next year, U.S. officials warn in new assessment," *The Washington Post*, July 25, 2017. (*https://www.washingtonpost.com/world/national-security/north-korea-could-cross-icbm-threshold-next-year-us-officials-warn-in-new-assessment/2017/07/25/4107dc4a-70af-11e7-8f39-eeb7d3a2d304-_story.html?nid&utm_term=.63b042018d2a*)

[4] Anna Fifield, "In latest test, North Korea detonates its most powerful nuclear device yet," *The Washington Post*, September 3, 2017. (*https://www.washingtonpost.com/world/north-korea-apparently-conducts-another-nuclear-test-south-korea-says/2017/09/03/7bce3ff6-905b-11e7-8df5-c2e5cf46c1e2_story.html?utm_term=.17217f662896*)

[5] Additional North Korea proliferation examples cited in: Anthony Ruggiero, "Restricting North Korea's Access to Finance," Testimony before House Committee on Financial Services, Subcommittee on Monetary Policy and Trade, July 19, 2017. (*http://www.defenddemocracy.org/content/uploads/documents/Anthony_Ruggiero_Testimony_HFSC.pdf*)

[6] U.S. Department of the Treasury, Press Release, "Treasury Sanctions Those Involved in Ballistic Missile Procurement for Iran," January 17, 2016. (*https://www.treasury.gov/press-center/press-releases/Pages/jl0322.aspx*)

[7] Jeff Daniels, "North Korea's 'No. 2' official strengthens ties with Iran as U.N. hits Pyongyang with new sanctions," *CNBC*, August 4, 2017. (*https://www.cnbc.com/2017/08/04/north-korea-officials-visit-to-iran-could-signal-wider-military-ties.html*)

[8] Anthony Ruggiero, "Gauging the North Korea-Iran Relationship," Foundation for Defense of Democracies, March 8, 2017. (*http://www.defenddemocracy.org/media-hit/anthony-ruggiero-gauging-the-north-korea-iran-relationship/*)

[9] Gregory L. Schulte, "Uncovering Syria's Covert Reactor," Carnegie Endowment for International Peace, January 2010. (*http://carnegieendowment.org/files/schulte_syria.pdf*); Robin

Continued

The lesson North Korea learned from its Syrian adventure was that once the United States has committed itself to "engagement," it loses the will to punish even the most blatant disregard for international norms. Even though North Korea built the Syrian reactor while at times pretending to engage in serious denuclearization talks, the Bush administration went ahead and removed North Korea from the state sponsor of terrorism list in 2008. Since North Korea was not punished for constructing a nuclear reactor in Syria, it will likely decide that scientific exchanges with Iran or other countries are not likely to be detectable and will not be subject to punishment even if they are discovered.

One should also note that North Korea's relationship with Syria included the transfer of materiel used for chemical weapons, which is especially disturbing given the Assad regime's use of chemical weapons on its own population. In 2009, Greece stopped a vessel headed to Syria that was suspected of violating North Korea-related U.N. sanctions; authorities found 13,000 chemical protective suits manufactured in North Korea.[10] In 2013, Turkey stopped a vessel that originated in North Korea; it was carrying 1,400 rifles and pistols, 30,000 rounds of ammunition, and gas masks destined for Syria.[11] The United Nations Panel of Experts noted in its September 2017 midterm report that it is investigating additional interdictions of North Korean-related vessels headed to Syria, as well as continued cooperation between Pyongyang and Damascus (including North Korean representatives in Syria), and a contract that could include cooperation on chemical weapons, ballistic missiles, and conventional arms.[12]

Another aspect of North Korea's proliferation activities is the role China and Russia play in allowing Pyongyang's proliferation entities to operate in their respective countries 11 years after the first U.N. sanctions were passed. Recent examples came to light when Treasury in early June sanctioned a Russian company and individual for providing supplies to Korea Tangun Trading Corporation and noted the individual is a frequent business partner of Tangun officials in Moscow.[13] Tangun was designated by the United States and United Nations in 2009 for its involvement in North Korea's WMD and missile programs. In late August, Russia's Gefest-M LLC and its director were sanctioned for procuring metals for Tangun's Moscow office.[14]

In late August, Treasury sanctioned a Chinese company, Dandong Rich Earth Trading Co., Ltd., that purchased vanadium ore from a U.N.- and U.S.-sanctioned company, Korea Kumsan Trading Corporation, which is tied directly to North Korea's nuclear weapons program.[15] The United Nations prohibited North Korea's exports of vanadium ore in March 2016.[16]

These examples highlighting Pyongyang's provocations extend beyond its nuclear weapons and missile tests to continued operations of its proliferation entities and transfer of nuclear-, chemical-, and missile-related items. It also underscores why we cannot fall back into a period of acceptance of these provocations and must use robust, Iran-style sanctions to limit these activities.

IRAN-STYLE SANCTIONS

North Korea says it is not interested in denuclearization, and its actions reinforce its words. Pyongyang showed us the "Map of Death" in 2013 suggesting its nuclear targets are Washington, DC; Hawaii, home to Pacific Command; possibly San Diego, home to the Pacific Fleet; and possibly San Antonio, home to U.S. Air Force Cyber Command.[17] Just after the July 4 ICBM test, North Korea's state media said that

---

Wright, "N. Koreans Taped At Syrian Reactor," *The Washington Post*, April 24, 2008. (*http://www.washingtonpost.com/wp-dyn/content/article/2008/04/23/AR2008042302906.html*)

[10] Joseph S. Bermudez Jr., "North Korea's Chemical Warfare Capabilities," 38 North, October 10, 2013. (*http://www.38north.org/2013/10/jbermudez101013/*)

[11] Barbara Demick, "North Korea tried to ship gas masks to Syria, report says," *The Los Angeles Times*, August 27, 2013. (*http://articles.latimes.com/2013/aug/27/world/la-fg-wn-north-korea-syria-gas-masks-20130827*)

[12] United Nations Security Council, "Midterm report of the Panel of Experts established pursuant to resolution 1874 (2009)," September 5, 2017. (*http://www.un.org/ga/search/view_doc.asp?symbol=S/2017/742*)

[13] U.S. Department of the Treasury, Press Release, "Treasury Sanctions Suppliers of North Korea's Nuclear and Weapons Proliferation Programs," June 1, 2017. (*https://www.treasury.gov/press-center/press-releases/Pages/sm0099.aspx*)

[14] U.S. Department of the Treasury, Press Release, "Treasury Targets Chinese and Russian Entities and Individuals Supporting the North Korean Regime," August 22, 2017. (*https://www.treasury.gov/press-center/press-releases/Pages/sm0148.aspx*)

[15] Ibid.

[16] United Nations Security Council, Resolution 2270, March 2, 2016. (*http://www.un.org/en/ga/search/view_doc.asp?symbol=S/RES/2270%282016%29*)

[17] Jeffrey Lewis, "The Map of Death," *Foreign Policy*, April 3, 2013. (*http://foreignpolicy.com/2013/04/03/the-map-of-death/*)

the Kim regime would not negotiate away its nuclear weapons or ballistic missiles or stop bolstering its nuclear force unless the United States ended its "hostile policy and nuclear threat" to North Korea.[18] Translation: When Washington abandons its allies in Tokyo and Seoul and removes all troops, North Korea might be willing to talk about its programs.

Rather than working to overcome Pyongyang's intransigence, many experts call for the acceptance of North Korea as a nuclear weapons state and insist that the United States can protect itself with a policy of deterrence.[19] Both nuclear and conventional deterrence are essential components of a comprehensive U.S. strategy, yet are not effective means of exerting pressure on Pyongyang or preventing dangerous provocations. Some suggest the United States has successfully deterred Pyongyang, since there has been no second Korean War. Nonetheless, North Korea's reckless behavior in recent years has included sinking the Cheonan, killing over 40 South Korean sailors, maintaining a robust relationship with Iran, building a nuclear reactor in Syria that Israel destroyed in 2007, and launching ballistic missiles directly over Japan. Unfortunately, this is a short list of the limits of deterrence.

Some experts suggest the policy of deterrence should be complemented by a freeze of North Korea's nuclear weapons and missile programs that will lead to a reduction of the threat and roll-back elements of the programs. Pyongyang has a history of pocketing the incentives it has been offered in exchange for temporary restraints, then violating the deals with great haste. While nominally abiding by the 1994 Agreed Framework, North Korea developed a covert uranium enrichment program. We discussed earlier how Israel destroyed a nuclear reactor in Syria built by North Korea during negotiations on its nuclear program.

The Trump administration is pursuing Iran-style sanctions to force North Korea to denuclearize and, absent that result, protect the United States and its allies from Pyongyang's activities. Both critics and supporters of the 2015 nuclear deal agree that sanctions were the main driver that brought Iran to the negotiating table. Last month I testified before the Senate Committee on Banking, Housing, and Urban Affairs, noting that before Congress passed the first North Korea sanctions law, sanctions against North Korea were not strong or well-enforced. Despite the misconception that North Korea is already the most-sanctioned country in the world, FDD's research shows that Pyongyang was the eighth most-sanctioned country in February 2016 and has moved up to fourth behind Ukraine/Russia, Syria, and Iran.[20]

The key aspect of the Iran sanctions model was that it forced companies, individuals, banks, and governments in the United States and abroad to make a choice: Stop doing business with Iran, or lose access to the U.S. dollar and risk the United States freezing their assets and labeling them as doing business with a state sponsor of terrorism intent on developing a nuclear weapon. The approach worked. Around the world, banks, and companies—and eventually governments—curtailed or eliminated business with Iran.[21]

Executive Order 13810, issued last month, is the latest in the Trump administration's efforts to clarify the choice for countries: Do business with North Korea or the United States, it cannot be both.[22] The approach combines diplomatic efforts to convince countries to cut ties with North Korea supported by the threat of losing access to the U.S. financial system. Those efforts are beginning to work as countries are

---

[18] "Kim Jong-un Supervises Test-launch of Inter-continental Ballistic Rocket Hwasong–14," Korean Central News Agency (North Korea), July 5, 2017. (*https://kcnawatch.co/newstream/276945/kim-jong-un-supervises-test-launch-of-inter-continental-ballistic-rocket-hwasong-14/*)

[19] Jimmy Carter, "Jimmy Carter: What I've learned from North Korea's leaders," *The Washington Post*, October 4, 2017. (*https://www.washingtonpost.com/opinions/jimmy-carter-what-ive-learned-from-north-koreas-leaders/2017/10/04/a2851a9e-a7bb-11e7-850e-2bdd1236be5d_-story.html?utm_term=.e5801c8b4261*); Fareed Zakaria, "There's a way out on North Korea," *The Washington Post*, September 28, 2017. (*https://www.washingtonpost.com/opinions/theres-a-way-out-on-north-korea/2017/09/28/4382dfc4-a48a-11e7-b14f-f41773cd5a14_story.html?-utm_term=.c0c3153afcc8)*; William J. Perry, "To confront North Korea, talk first and get tough later," *The Washington Post*, January 6, 2017. (*https://www.washingtonpost.com/opinions/to-confront-north-korea-talk-first-and-get-tough-later/2017/01/06/9334aee4-d451-11e6-9cb0-54ab630851e8_story.html?utm_term=.68cb376d8927*)

[20] Anthony Ruggiero, "Evaluating Sanctions Enforcement and Policy Options on North Korea," Testimony before Senate Committee on Banking, Housing, and Urban Affairs, September 7, 2017. (*http://www.defenddemocracy.org/content/uploads/documents/09-07-17_AR_Senate_-Banking_Testimony-1.pdf*)

[21] Paul Sonne and Felicia Schwartz, "U.S. Pressure on North Korea's Global Ties Bears Fruit," The Wall Street Journal, October 8, 2017. (*https://www.wsj.com/articles/State-department-pressure-on-north-koreas-global-ties-bears-fruit-1507492004*)

[22] Executive Order 13810, "Imposing Additional Sanctions With Respect to North Korea," September 20, 2017. (*https://www.treasury.gov/resource-center/sanctions/Programs/Documents/13810.pdf*)

choosing America's $19-trillion economy. The *Wall Street Journal* reported that a year-long effort by the State Department resulted in over 20 countries cutting off diplomatic or commercial relationships with North Korea.

China will play a large role in an effective, Iran-style sanctions regime against North Korea, given Beijing's robust economic relationship with Pyongyang. Over the last decade, Republican and Democratic presidents have pressed China's leadership to implement tough sanctions against North Korea, hoping the approach would be effective. But Beijing continued to vote for tough U.N. sanctions it has not implemented, and allowed its firms, individuals, and banks to facilitate North Korea's sanctions evasion.

The Trump administration has started to address the problem directly by targeting Chinese banks that process financial transactions through the U.S. financial system on behalf of North Korea and Chinese networks that profit from facilitating North Korea's sanctions evasion. In particular, the Trump administration has used the Justice and Treasury Departments to sanction a Chinese bank, individuals, and firms; request that Federal courts return assets illegally processed through the U.S. financial system; and request additional fines.[23]

In late September, Treasury sanctioned 26 North Korean banking representatives, including 19 in China; a clear message to Beijing and its banks that it must clean up its act or face consequences.[24] Chinese leadership has responded to this pressure with the People's Bank of China, its central bank, issuing a directive mandating banks stop transactions with North Koreans.[25]

But Beijing must do more to ensure North Korea cannot use China as a hub for its sanctions evasion. Chinese banks should increase scrutiny of financial and commercial relationships to identify and stop transactions with North Korea. Chinese banks have the financial resources to do it, but the Trump administration likely will need to sanction additional Chinese banks to reinforce the message, starting with fines similar to the approach against European banks for Iran sanctions violations.

DHS ROLE IN SANCTIONS

In prior testimonies, I detailed flaws in the current sanctions regime, including not prioritizing the North Korea sanctions program and the need to focus on Pyongyang's overseas business network and non-North Koreans facilitating sanctions evasion.[26] North Korea's shipping network plays a crucial role in Pyongyang's sanctions evasion, including the prohibited transfer of commodities.

---

[23] Six actions against China show a developing pattern: 1) May 22: damming warrants against Dandong Zhicheng network requiring eight U.S. banks to freeze U.S. dollar transactions; 2) June 14: asset forfeiture request for $1.9 million from Mingzheng; 3) June 29: declaring a Chinese bank (Bank of Dandong) a money launderer for North Korea; 4) June 29: designation of two Chinese individuals and entity; 5) August 22: designation of five Chinese firms and one individual, including Dandong Zhicheng network; and 6) August 22: asset forfeiture request from the Dandong Zhicheng network. *United States of America* v. *All Wire Transactions Involving Dandong Zhicheng Metallic Material Company, LTD., et. al.* (D.D.C. filed May 22, 2017). (*http://www.dcd.uscourts.gov/sites/dcd/files/BAHMemoandOrder.pdf*); *United States of America* v. *Funds Associated with Mingzheng International Trading Limited,* No. 1:17-cv-01166-KBJ (D.D.C. June 14, 2017). (Accessed via PACER); Proposal of Special Measure Against Bank of Dandong as a Financial Institution of Primary Money Laundering Concern, U.S. Department of the Treasury, Financial Crimes Enforcement Network, 82 Federal Register 31537, July 7, 2017. (*https://www.fincen.gov/sites/default/files/Federal_register_notices/2017-07-07/2017-14026.pdf*); U.S. Department of the Treasury, Press Release, "Treasury Acts to Increase Economic Pressure on North Korea and Protect the U.S. Financial System," June 29, 2017. (*https://www.treasury.gov/press-center/press-releases/Pages/sm0118.aspx*); U.S. Department of the Treasury, Press Release, "Treasury Targets Chinese and Russian Entities and Individuals Supporting the North Korean Regime," August 22, 2017. (*https://www.treasury.gov/press-center/press-releases/Pages/sm0148.aspx*); *United States of America* v. *Funds Associated with Dandong Chengtai Trading Limited,* No. 1:17-cv-01706 (D.D.C. August 22, 2017). (Accessed via PACER)

[24] U.S. Department of the Treasury, Press Release, "Treasury Sanctions Banks and Representatives Linked to North Korean Financial Networks," September 26, 2017. (*https://www.treasury.gov/press-center/press-releases/Pages/sm0165.aspx*)

[25] "China's central bank tells banks to stop doing business with North Korea: sources," Reuters, September 21, 2017. (*http://www.reuters.com/article/us-northkorea-missiles-banks-china/chinas-central-bank-tells-banks-to-stop-doing-business-with-north-korea-sources-idUSKCN1BW-1DL?il=0*)

[26] Anthony Ruggiero, "Restricting North Korea's Access to Finance," Testimony before House Committee on Financial Services, Subcommittee on Monetary Policy and Trade, July 19, 2017. (*http://www.defenddemocracy.org/content/uploads/documents/Anthony_Ruggiero_Testimony-_HFSC.pdf*); Anthony Ruggiero, "Evaluating Sanctions Enforcement and Policy Options on North Korea," Testimony before Senate Committee on Banking, Housing, and Urban Affairs, September 7, 2017. (*http://www.defenddemocracy.org/content/uploads/documents/09-07-17_AR_Senate_Banking_Testimony-1.pdf*)

The Countering America's Adversaries Through Sanctions Act (CAASA) contains several provisions for the Department of Homeland Security that will highlight the role of North Korean vessels in illicit transfers and the role of countries that facilitate these transfers.[27]

CAASA amends the Ports and Waterways Safety Act by requiring the Secretary of Homeland Security to publish a list of vessels "owned or operated by or on behalf of the Government of North Korea or a North Korean person."[28] Even though Treasury's Office of Foreign Assets Control currently lists only 40 vessels as blocked property of North Korean-designated persons, FDD research indicates that more than 140 could be linked to North Korea. The Department of Homeland Security, in consultation with other relevant agencies, should take an expansive view of the legal requirement to name North Korean-linked vessels, including those owned and/or managed by non-North Korean front companies. Pyongyang has extensive experience hiding its involvement in the commercial and financial sectors, a practice that likely extends to the shipping sector.

The law requires the list to contain vessels owned by countries: (1) Whose sea ports are not implementing U.N. shipping sanctions or facilitate the transfer of cargo prohibited by the United Nations; and (2) are identified by the president as not complying with applicable U.N. sanctions.[29] This provision will be crucial, as China and Russia have allowed North Korean-linked vessels to continue to transfer prohibited materials. Beijing and Moscow will need to increase their inspection of North Korea-linked vessels to ensure compliance with U.N. shipping sanctions, including verifying Pyongyang is not importing or exporting prohibited materiel or commodities. Treasury Assistant Secretary Marshall Billingslea highlighted this challenge in testimony on September 12 before the House Foreign Affairs Committee. Billingslea noted that North Korean vessels transferred North Korean coal to China after turning off its vessel identification systems, a highly suspicious action. North Korean vessels have also used Russian ports to transfer North Korean coal between vessels to further obscure its shipment to China.[30]

The Department of Homeland Security and other elements of the U.S. Government must focus on the activities of North Korean-linked vessels, including increasing the number of entities and individuals sanctioned in North Korea's shipping sector, compiling a complete listing of vessels linked to North Korea, and naming ports in China and Russia that facilitate North Korea's sanctions evasion. The urgency of the threat calls for the Department to take these actions before the 180-day period granted by CAASA has elapsed.

CONCLUSION

North Korea's nuclear weapons and missile programs are a threat to the U.S. homeland and our allies. There are two policy options: One accepts this dangerous situation as reality under the false premise that North Korea's provocations can be contained or deterred. The other path was successful in bringing Iran to the negotiating table with crushing sanctions that could force the Kim regime to realize the futility of continuing its nuclear weapons and missile programs. The only peaceful way to protect the U.S. homeland is to ensure Kim Jong-un feels the full weight of sanctions implemented by the United States and our allies.

On behalf of the Foundation for Defense of Democracies, I thank you again for inviting me to testify and I look forward to addressing your questions.

Mr. PERRY. The Chair thanks the gentleman.

The Chair now recognizes Mr. Terrell for an opening statement.

STATEMENT OF PATRICK R. TERRELL, SENIOR RESEARCH FELLOW, CENTER FOR THE STUDY OF WEAPONS OF MASS DESTRUCTION, NATIONAL DEFENSE UNIVERSITY

Mr. TERRELL. Chairman Perry, Ranking Member Correa, distinguished Members of the subcommittee, it is my honor today to tes-

---

[27] Countering America's Adversaries Through Sanctions Act, 115 U.S.C. (*https://www.whitehouse.gov/legislation/hr-3364-countering-americas-adversaries-through-sanctions-act*)

[28] Ibid.

[29] Ibid.

[30] Marshall Billingslea, "Sanctions, Diplomacy, and Information: Pressuring North Korea," Testimony before House Foreign Affairs Committee, September 12, 2017. (*http://docs.house.gov/meetings/FA/FA00/20170912/106389/HHRG-115-FA00-WState-BillingsleaM-20170912.pdf*)

tify on the North Korean WMD threats to the homeland. The views expressed in this testimony are my own and do not reflect those of the National Defense University or the Department of Defense.

We do not yet face a clear and present existential threat to the American homeland from North Korea, but it is getting closer each day. The threat will be very real very shortly, but it is nevertheless potentially manageable.

Today, North Korea possesses nuclear, chemical, and potentially biological weapons that can be unleashed directly or through others against U.S. vital interests abroad and in the homeland.

Under Kim Jong-il and Kim Jong-un—or Kim Il-sung and Kim Jong-il, nuclear weapons development progressed at a steady pace, a very deliberate pace. With Kim Jong-un, we have seen this extreme increase in pace of intermediate and intercontinental ballistic missile testing and nuclear weapons testing, to include the most recent one in September. This acceleration has North Korea on the verge of a functional road-mobile ICBM capable of delivering nuclear weapons to the continental United States.

While questions remain about the overall trajectory of the program, North Korea could have, by some estimates, enough fissile material for up to 60 nuclear weapons. Not all of those will be their most sophisticated design, but they could still be employed. Whatever miniaturized warheads they have managed to manufacture to this point could be used against Guam and the continental United States. While the reliability, accuracy, and survivability is questionable, we should expect that North Korea could endeavor to use these weapons in a time of crisis.

Additionally, North Korea maintains a large stockpile of chemical warfare agents, probably mostly consisting of blister and nerve agents which, while intended for warfighting, the Korean geography supports strategic employment against the 25 million people living in the greater Seoul metropolitan area, which would almost assuredly result in exposure to some of the 140,000 American citizens living in South Korea, and raise the potential for the need of returned chemical casualties to United States for long-term care.

The assassination of Kim Jong-nam with VX in Kuala Lumpur this February demonstrated North Korea's ability to transport and use chemical weapons overseas. While we know far less about their biological weapons program, it is believed that given the infrastructure that they possess within North Korea, they can conduct research and development and possibly produce small batches of biological agents.

North Korea's long history of shipping conventional arms, drugs, and counterfeit money could facilitate attempts to move chemical or biological weapons into the U.S. homeland for attack. While not on the scale achievable in South Korea, they could be impactful enough to foment fear. While no one has clear insights into Kim Jong-un's thinking, we can surmise he has two primary objectives: His personal survival and the continued existence of a Kim-led regime. To that end, watching Iraq and Libya could reinforce his belief that he is more likely to remain in power by demonstrating a credible operational WMD capability intended to deter attack on the Korean peninsula.

We also know North Korea remains intent on breaking our alliance system in Asia, and believes that threats to the homeland will cause United States to abandon South Korea and Japan during a time of crisis. We also know that both Kim Jong-un and his father believed they could manage provocations in the escalation, and that by possessing a nuclear weapon, he believes that the U.S. threshold for war may be heightened, allowing him to be more provocative and belligerent.

So what can we do about this? The pressure campaign must remain global. We must strengthen our homeland and develop a modern approach to deterrence. Regional economic links and military posture are essential to demonstrating U.S. presence as a transpacific leader. Financial diplomatic and informational pressures in other regions of the world must be applied to cut off potential trading partners.

Next, the United States must protect all of our territory from North Korean attacks and respond should one occur. Many of the actions the Department of Defense, Department of Homeland Security, and others have taken to prepare for WMD attack by terrorists would also apply to North Korean attacks against the homeland. We must enhance our nuclear preparedness to include planning for and exercising responses to large-scale attacks, perhaps with multiple nuclear weapons.

I am not sure we have fully grasped how difficult the logistics and coordination will be for immediate life-saving actions, short-term relief efforts, and long-term rebuilding following multiple nuclear detonations, particularly if one is 2,500 miles away in Hawaii or over 6,000 miles away in Guam.

Finally, we need to tailor a deterrent approach for the unique challenge of North Korea. Kim Jong-un must understand that any conflict with the United States will end his regime and he will be denied the effects he is seeking to achieve. He should see how his nuclear threats strengthen our alliance. Resolve is demonstrated not by words, but by deeds: Proper resourcing, training, and exercising of our response forces; demonstrating our ballistic missile defenses; hardening our critical infrastructure against attack; and possessing a ready, reliable, and survivable nuclear triad.

Again, thank you for this opportunity, and I look forward to your questions.

[The prepared statement of Mr. Terrell follows:]

PREPARED STATEMENT OF PATRICK R. TERRELL

OCTOBER 12, 2017

Chairman Perry, Ranking Member Correa, and distinguished Members of the subcommittee: It is my honor to testify on the weapons of mass destruction threat posed to the United States by North Korea. The views expressed in this testimony are my own and do not reflect those of the National Defense University or the Department of Defense.

As to the seriousness of the dangers posed by the North Korean WMD arsenal to the U.S. homeland I would say, "We do not yet face a clear and present existential threat to the American homeland, but we are getting closer each day. The threat will be very real very shortly—but it is nevertheless potentially manageable if we take the appropriate steps."

North Korea is not a new threat that has suddenly developed; the United States has been dealing with North Korea for 67 years. For most of that time, the challenges posed by North Korea remained isolated to the Korean peninsula and northeast Asia. Then particularly after the fall of the Soviet Union, North Korean arms sales particularly in the Middle East and African turned them into a global proliferation concern aiding other rogue regimes, such as Syria and Iran. With respect to North Korean WMD development, the North Korean leadership has long recognized the conventional military advantage the United States-Republic of Korea alliance maintains on the land, in the sea, and in the air. Therefore, Kim Il-Sung looked to develop asymmetric advantages, first through the development of chemical and possibly biological weapons, and subsequently through its extensive nuclear and missile programs.

NUCLEAR

Over the past 40 years, North Korea has invested heavily in the development of ballistic missiles and nuclear weapons as a strategic capability. Additionally, the ballistic missile program provides real warfighting capabilities and a commodity that generates income for the State and the nuclear weapons program through sales to a myriad of countries to include Syria and Iran.

In May 2016, Kim Jong-un established the nuclear weapons program and economic growth as the two pillars of North Korean strength.[1] Under Kim Jong-un's leadership, North Korea's intermediate range ballistic missiles (IRBM) and intercontinental ballistic missile (ICBM) testing has increased in frequency and success. While it may seem like a normal action for a nation to "develop, test, verify, and then field" a missile program, it is a shift for North Korea, which had previously fielded entire systems with little or no testing. Such a shift marks a change from North Korea being concerned about the appearance of its missile programs to being concerned about its efficacy of its missiles. The takeaway from the 77 tests since January 2014 (compared to 36 in the preceding 29 years) is that Kim Jong-un, unlike his father, has not been afraid to fail, sometimes even catastrophically, which has been the key to learning and advancement in the missile program in order to reach key operational thresholds.[2]

For many years under Kim Il-sung and Kim Jong-il, the nuclear weapons development process moved along at a deliberate pace. This offered opportunities for the United States to attempt to negotiate a halt to its progress through trade-offs and incentives. The nuclear tests in 2006 and 2009 acted as an inflection point in the international community's efforts to halt the nuclear program. Since Kim Jong-un has taken power, North Korea has conducted four tests, with the September 3, 2017 test having a yield of roughly 140 kilotons, or nearly ten times larger than the bomb dropped on Hiroshima.[3]

These recent and successful ballistic missile and nuclear weapons tests suggest that North Korea is close to completing the development of a functional road-mobile ICBM capable of delivering a nuclear warhead to the continental United States. There are still several questions about the program ranging from "how many ICBMs does Kim Jong-un plan to build", to "how will North Korea control and safeguard the arsenal", and "will North Korean behavior change". We should remember that North Korea has been working at this for quite some time and while estimates range from 10 to 12 weapons to 30 to 60 weapon, the important point is Kim Jong-un is beyond having a weapon he can brandish, but now has a growing stockpile and he will develop a doctrine to employ it.[4][5] Not all weapons will use their most sophisticated designs, but it is almost a certainty that, if it chooses, North Korea can employ nuclear weapons today. This use could take multiple forms, such as defensively within North Korea or on short-range missiles against targets in South Korea or Japan or by cargo ship or plane to other locations within the surrounding region. North Korea could use whatever miniaturized warheads they have on intermediate range Hwasong–12 IRBMs capable of reaching Guam or on Hwasong–14 ICBMs capable of reaching the Continental United States. While the reliability, accuracy, and survivability upon reentry of the fully-mated system is questionable,

[1] James Pearson, "North Korea Leader Kim Sets Five-Year Economic Plan, Vows Nuclear Restraint," *Reuters*, May 8, 2016, *http://www.reuters.com/article/us-northkorea-congress-idUSKCN0XY0QB*.

[2] Nuclear Threat Initiative, *The North Korean Missile Test Tracker*, *http://www.nti.org/analysis/articles/cns-north-korea-missile-test-database/*, accessed October 10, 2017.

[3] Panda, Ankit, "US Intelligence: North Korea's Sixth Test Was a 140 Kiloton 'Advanced Nuclear' Device", *The Diplomat*, September 6, 2017, *https://thediplomat.com/2017/09/us-intelligence-north-koreas-sixth-test-was-a-140-kiloton-advanced-nuclear-device/*.

[4] Deb Riechmann and Matthew Pennington, "Here's Why It's Hard to Pin Down the Actual Size of North Korea's Nuclear Arsenal", *Time*, August 18, 2017, *http://time.com/4906219/north-korea-nuclear-weapons-how-many/*.

[5] Shane Smith, "North Korea's Nuclear Futures Series: North Korea's Evolving Nuclear Strategy", AUGUST 2015, *http://www.38north.org/2015/08/nukefuture082415/*.

North Korea could still mount and attempt to deliver such munitions in times of crisis.

CHEMICAL

North Korea maintains a large, operationally-ready stockpile of persistent and non-persistent chemical warfare agents capable of delivery via artillery, rockets, missiles, and aerial bombs. The program probably consists of the traditional chemical warfare agents mustard, lewisite, and both G-series and V-series nerve agents and fits the profile of a warfighting chemical weapons program intended for defensive and offensive employment along the demilitarized zone and against U.S. and ROK airbases and seaports to halt or slow down the flow of reinforcements and logistics.[6] [7] The geography of the Korean peninsula allows for a strategic employment of chemical weapons against unprotected civilians by long-range artillery in the Kaesong Heights against the 25 million people in Seoul and by ballistic missiles further north against other South Korean cities, such as Busan. This type of chemical weapons use by North Korea during a conflict in Northeast Asia would almost assuredly result in casualties to some of the 140,000 American citizens living in the Republic of Korea. These casualties would be not only U.S. Service Members, but also family members, Americans working abroad and traveling as tourists. The total number of civilians the United States could be required to evacuate could swell to 230,000, with some being potentially chemical casualties requiring transportation to the United States for long-term care. While the military would do everything possible to prevent the unintentional transfer of contaminated materials to the United States, there will be a need for close coordination with Customs and Border Protection, the Environmental Protection Agency, and State regulators.

Of particular interest to the Departments of Homeland Security, Commerce, State, and Justice is the latest development regarding North Korea's chemical weapons program—and most brazen proof of the program's existence: The use of VX nerve agent to assassinate Kim Jong-nam in Kuala Lumpur, Malaysia on February 13, 2017. This attack indicates a willingness to use chemical weapons in unconventional ways and an ability to transport chemical agents across borders without being caught.[8] North Korea has a long-established history of using front companies and their embassies to proliferate conventional arms, drugs, and counterfeit money. North Korea could use these same connections to transport chemical weapons through the Middle East, Africa, or South America to agents in the U.S. homeland or to sell chemical weapons to violent extremists who could then attack American interests globally. While North Korea's goal presumably would be to achieve a greater impact than a single assassination, they would not be able to achieve an attack in any way close to the scale of massed artillery fire into Seoul; however, they could still disrupt daily American life, and create mass panic and fear.

BIOLOGICAL

We know far less about North Korea's biological weapons program. Even though it is a member of the Biological and Toxins Weapons Convention, it is believed to maintain the ability to conduct research and possibly produce some small amounts of biological agents.[9] Attempts by North Korea to smuggle biological agents into the United States would be challenging. Unlike chemical weapons, where the chief concern of the smuggler is with the shipping container breaking or leaking, with biological pathogens the virus or bacteria must be kept alive during transportation. A viable biological agent dissemination method must also be available. Biological agents, particularly toxins, have proven useful in assassinations, but to date they have not proven to be effective, nor necessarily sought after, for large-scale attacks.

NORTH KOREAN RATIONALE FOR WMD

When considering the threat posed, it is important to understand why North Korea believes they need weapons of mass destruction. While no one possess reliable insight into what or how Kim Jong-un thinks, we can reasonably surmise that his

---

[6] "North Korea: Chemical Program," Nuclear Threat Initiative, Last modified December 2015, *http://www.nti.org/learn/countries/north-korea/chemical/*.

[7] Emma Chanlett-Avery et. al, "North Korea: U.S. Relations, Nuclear Diplomacy, and Internal Situation," Congressional Research Service, January 15, 2016, pg. 13.

[8] Executive Council Decision (EC–84/DEC.8), Organization for the Prohibition of Chemical Weapons (OPCW), March 9, 2017, *https://www.opcw.org/fileadmin/OPCW/EC/84/en/ec84dec08_e_.pdf*.

[9] North Korea: Biological Program, Nuclear Threat Initiative, December 2015, *http://www.nti.org/learn/countries/north-korea/biological/*.

primary objective remains—and will remain—his personal survival and the continued existence of a Kim-led regime. To that end, watching the demise of Saddam Hussain and Muammar Gaddafi could have led him to believe that he is more likely to remain in power by retaining an operational nuclear and chemical weapons capability to deter attack by the Republic of Korea and the United States. In order for North Korea to establish a deterrent, it must demonstrate a credible capability consisting of accurate and reliable missiles fitted with functional nuclear warheads. In the North Korean view, the fielding of this capability will change past rhetoric about attacking the United States into a real deterrent message. Therefore, we should not expect Kim Jong-un to halt his development until he feels he has adequate weapons systems to impose enough cost on the United States that we will not attempt a regime change. Since this is all about his perception of a U.S. threshold, he may have no realistic view of what size arsenal he needs. Therefore, it is difficult to predict how many nuclear weapons North Korea could eventually possess.

Next, we know North Korea is intent on decoupling the United States from the Republic of Korea and ultimately breaking the U.S.-ROK alliance. Kim Jong-un likely believes that by placing our homeland at risk, the United States will abandon South Korea should a conflict arise, or at least be too pre-occupied with homeland defense to adequately reinforce the Korean peninsula. To support this effort, North Korea has released propaganda videos showing attacks against major U.S. cities and key military bases. They understand the military utility in preventing U.S. forces from reaching Korea and they believe that the U.S. Government is unwilling to trade Los Angeles or Seattle for Seoul. While there have been countless heinous acts committed by the Kim dynasty, in retrospect its foreign policy over the past 20 years has proven to have a certain rationality. Kim Jong-il used provocations to garner international assistance and Kim Jong-un uses provocations to shore up domestic support. Both father and son believed they could manage the level of escalation and end the provocation cycle before crossing a threshold that would lead to war. From Kim Jong-un's perspective, he may believe possessing nuclear weapons raises the U.S. threshold for war and allows him political space to engage in greater provocative actions in the region. Therefore, it is very possible that the United States will face an even more emboldened and belligerent North Korea.

Given these assumptions on North Korea's strategic aims and views on provocations, the challenge becomes, "What will lead to North Korean WMD employment and what does this mean for homeland security? Will Kim Jong-un only use nuclear weapons in a first strike and if so what indications will we have that he is planning an attack? What will be Kim Jong-un's priority targets for nuclear weapons employment?" Aspects of these answers are tied to how the United States reacts to the threat.

SO WHAT CAN THE UNITED STATES DO?

The U.S. approach must be multi-faceted and include global isolation of North Korea, a strengthened homeland, and a modern approach to deterrence. Beginning overseas, the United States economic links and military posture are essential to demonstrate to North Korea and our allies U.S. permanency as a trans-Pacific leader. While sanctions against North Korean elites are important to raising pressure inside Pyongyang, financial, diplomatic, and informational pressure must be applied to cut off potential licit and illicit trading partners around the world. The Kim regime provides ample evidence that the United States can use to influence all legitimate governments or businesses to choose to forego any commercial or political support of North Korea.

Next, the United States must be prepared to protect all of our territory from a North Korean attack and respond should one occur. Ballistic missile defense is an important part of our overall strategy as it provides a layer of protection, but as with any shield, it is not perfect. The technological challenges associated with shooting down missiles in flight and the shear scope of trying to stay ahead of a rapidly-growing threat are enormous. This is an area that I know garners a lot of attention in both the House and Senate and I admit to not being an expert in this field, so I encourage you to meet with the right experts on what more can or should be done.

Many of the actions the United States has taken domestically to prepare for the risks associated with a terrorist chemical or biological weapons attack would also help in the event of a covert attack by North Korea. However, we should continue to review and enhance our nuclear preparedness posture. For instance, our current preparedness planning assumes single small-scale terrorist devices; we should plan for and exercise responses to larger-scale attacks, perhaps with multiple nuclear weapons, that would quickly overwhelm our ability to manage the consequences of such a campaign. We saw how difficult it was to respond to the three hurricanes that recently struck U.S. territory only weeks apart. While it is easy to say, "America can do anything", I am not sure we have really grasped how difficult it would be to deal with three nuclear detonations on the homeland. This response would require a level of Federal, State, and local coordination never seen before. A different yet equally difficult response would be an attack against Guam or Hawaii. Responses to either of these islands would require immediate life-saving actions, short-term relief efforts and long-term rebuilding. All three of those areas can easily be crippled by the realities of time, distance, and the limitation of moving most logistics by ship.

As with past and current deterrence challenges, such as with the Soviet Union during the cold war and Russia and China today, the United States should take this threat seriously, but not overreact. We have to tailor our deterrent approach to the unique challenge North Korea poses with nuclear, chemical, and potentially biological weapons programs capable of being employed against U.S. vital interests both abroad and in the homeland. Global isolation, ballistic missile defense, and domestic preparedness are all vital to deterring North Korea. Kim Jong-un must understand that any conflict with the United States or our allies will cost him the things he holds most valuable and that the United States will deny him the effects he seeks to achieve. Rather than seeing nuclear threats against the United States as a means to separate our alliances, he should see how it strengthens our alliances and our resolve. Such resolve is demonstrated not with words, but by deeds: Proper resourcing, training, and exercising of our response force; exercising our local, State, and National response frameworks; demonstrating our ballistic missile defenses; ensuring that our critical infrastructure is hardened against the effects of a nuclear attack; and finally possessing a ready, reliable, and survivable nuclear triad.

Chairman Duncan, Ranking Member Correa, thank you for the opportunity to share my views with the subcommittee and I look forward to your questions.

Mr. PERRY. The Chair thanks Mr. Terrell.

The Chair now recognizes Mr. Greene for an opening statement.

STATEMENT OF JEFF GREENE, SENIOR DIRECTOR, GLOBAL GOVERNMENT AFFAIRS AND POLICY, SYMANTEC CORPORATION

Mr. GREENE. Chairman Perry, Ranking Member Correa, thank you for the opportunity to be here today.

We have been tracking the Lazarus Group, which the U.S. Government has linked to North Korea for over 5 years, and have watched as their targets have evolved and their technical skills have improved. Lazarus is different from other attack groups that have been linked to nation-states in several ways.

First, their attacks are unusual both in the breadth of their targets and in the goals of the attack itself. Second, Lazarus shows little hesitation to engage in activity that other groups might take pause. Finally, Lazarus targets a variety of disparate industries, many simultaneously, and is very quick to move from target to target. Their technical capabilities have improved dramatically over the past few years, and we view them as above average in overall capability and actually expert in some areas. In particular, their skill to conducting reconnoissance operations, and the quality of the malware that they developed has improved dramatically in the past few years.

The combination of this increased quality malware and new steps they have been taking in operational security will likely make it harder in the future to connect operations back to Lazarus.

In other areas, though, Lazarus has made fairly simple mistakes that have at times hampered their ability to complete an operation. These are usually, however, relatively basic, and we don't expect to see them making the mistakes in the future, given their demonstrated adaptability.

They have been connected to attacks in a wide variety of sectors from the entertainment industry, to critical infrastructure, to Government systems, to the financial sector and to the defense base. Unlike other groups that have been publicly connected to nation-states, Lazarus has attacked individual internet users en masse. Their methods run the gamut, and includes denial-of-service, highly targeted and sophisticated intrusions, destructive attacks, and the use of ransomware.

You both mentioned in your opening statement the theft of $81 million dollars from the Bangladesh Central Bank in 2016, but that is only part of the story. They actually targeted as much as a billion dollars, and but for a fairly simple mistake might have gotten away with it. They exploited weaknesses in the bank's security to infiltrate the network and steal credentials and then initiated fraudulent transfers. This was a well-planned and sophisticated attack.

To cover their tracks, they installed malware, which printed doctored confirmation receipts, so the folks in Bangladesh didn't know what was going on. The fraud was detected because they actually misspelled the names of the recipients of one of the fraudulent transfers, which led to inquiries.

Another Lazarus connected attack is the WannaCry ransomware outbreak that happened in May. This was fairly significant. Within the first hours, the National Health Service in the United Kingdom was taken down and the Spanish telecom provider Telefonica was impacted. WannaCry itself was unique and dangerous because it propagated autonomously. It was the first ransomware as a worm that has had global impact.

But while WannaCry was very good at infecting computers and encrypting data, it was really bad at collecting ransom. Because of some fairly simple coding errors, the attackers as yet do not appear to have actually collected the ransom that was paid by some of the victims.

Finally, you both mentioned, I believe, the Sony attack. This is probably the best-known Lazarus incident out there. It was late 2014, they were hit with malware that disabled networks, destroyed data, and stole emails. Most of the media attention after this was focused on the salaries of respective movie stars and other salacious details. But from a cybersecurity standpoint, the big story here was the permanent destruction in the United States of a significant number of computers and servers. By one report, the attack impacted as much as three-quarters of Sony's systems in Sony Pictures' headquarters. The FBI, as you probably know, and the DNI attributed this attack to the North Korean government. Our technical analysis has linked Sony to numerous other attacks, including the Bangladesh bank heist, WannaCry ransomware, Dark Soul, which was destructive attacks in Korea in 2011, the Polish bank heist that Mr. Cilluffo mentioned.

In sum, Lazarus is an aggressive and increasingly sophisticated attack group that has a demonstrated willingness to disrupt networks, steal money, and destroy computers and data. Unlike other major attack groups, which typically focus on one sector or even one industry, Lazarus has shown no such limitations. As a result, everyone has to assume that they could be a target of Lazarus and prepare accordingly.

Thank you for the opportunity to be here, and I am happy to take any questions.

[The prepared statement of Mr. Greene follows:]

PREPARED STATEMENT OF JEFF GREENE

OCTOBER 12, 2017

Chairman Perry, Chairman McCaul, Ranking Member Correa, Ranking Member Thompson, my name is Jeff Greene and I am the senior director, global government affairs and policy at Symantec. I am responsible for Symantec's global public policy agenda and government engagement strategy, and represent the company in key public policy initiatives and partnerships. I also serve as a member of the National Institute of Standards and Technology's (NIST) Information Security and Privacy Advisory Board (ISPAB), and recently supported the President's Commission on Enhancing National Cybersecurity. I have worked on the House and Senate Homeland Security Committees, and immediately prior to joining Symantec I served as senior counsel with the Senate committee focusing on cybersecurity and homeland defense issues.

Symantec Corporation is the world's leading cybersecurity company, and has the largest civilian threat collection network in the world. Our Global Intelligence Network™ tracks over 700,000 global adversaries and is comprised of more than 98 million attack sensors, which record thousands of events every second. This network monitors over 175 million endpoints located in over 157 countries and territories. Additionally, we process more than 2 billion emails and over 2.4 billion web requests each day. We maintain nine Security Response Centers and six Security Operations Centers around the globe, and all of these resources combined give our analysts a unique view of the entire cyber threat landscape.

Symantec has been tracking the Lazarus group for over 5 years, and we have watched as their targets have evolved and their technical skills have improved. Over the years we have linked numerous attacks to Lazarus, including the attack on Sony Pictures, the Bangladesh Central bank heist, and the recent WannaCry ransomware outbreak. The United States Government has publicly attributed the attack on Sony to the Democratic People's Republic of Korea.

In my testimony I will provide an assessment of the Lazarus group's technical capabilities and provide an overview of several attacks that we have connected to them. As an initial matter, however, I want to offer a few high-level observations on Lazarus:

- First, their attacks are unusual both in the breadth of their targets and the goals of their attacks.
- Second, Lazarus shows little hesitation to engage in activity that might give other attack groups pause.
- Finally, Lazarus targets a variety of disparate sectors, many simultaneously, and is very quick to move from target to target.

Lazarus' technical capabilities have improved dramatically in recent years, and we now view them as above-average in overall skills, and expert in some areas. In particular, Lazarus has shown excellent skills when conducting reconnaissance and researching operations, and over the past 3 to 4 years the quality of the malware they are producing has increased dramatically. Higher-quality malware is harder to detect, and this coupled with Lazarus' improving operational security steps could make it harder to connect future attacks with the group. The group is also a prolific developer of malware—while other highly sophisticated attack groups have a tendency to rely on a single malware family for a sustained campaign, Lazarus is more likely to use a unique (but less complex) piece of malware for each effort without concern for it being discovered within a shorter time frame so long as they achieve a specific end.

In other areas, Lazarus has shown a lack of overall ability that has at time hampered its ability to complete an operation successfully. Specifically, the WannaCry attacks yielded no apparent financial gain because the collection component was not set up properly, and the attack on the Bangladesh Central Bank was discovered and halted due to a typographical error. Unfortunately, these are relatively simple errors to correct and given Lazarus' ability to adapt and improve in recent years they are unlikely to repeat them in future operations.

Lazarus has been connected to attacks on a wide variety of sectors—from the entertainment industry to critical infrastructure to government systems to the financial sector. And unlike other groups that have been publicly connected to nation-states, Lazarus has attacked individual end-users of the internet. Lazarus' methods have also run the gamut, and include denial-of-service attacks, highly targeted (and highly sophisticated) intrusions, destructive attacks, and the use of ransomware. Below I will address three specific campaigns.

BANGLADESH CENTRAL BANK THEFT

In early 2016, Lazarus stole $81 million from Bangladesh's central bank—and but for a typographical error might have made off with as much as $1 billion. They exploited weaknesses in the bank's security to infiltrate its network and steal its Society for Worldwide Interbank Financial Telecommunication (SWIFT) credentials, allowing them to initiate fraudulent transfers (it is important to recognize that SWIFT itself was not compromised; the attackers used stolen credentials to initiate fraudulent transactions).

This was a well-planned, sophisticated attack: In order to cover their tracks, the attackers used malware to doctor the bank's printed confirmation messages to delay discovery of the transfers. They also began their attack at the start of a long weekend to reduce further the likelihood of a quick discovery. Once they obtained the bank's SWIFT credentials, the group made several transfer requests to the Federal Reserve Bank of New York for it to transfer the Bangladesh bank's money, primarily to locations in the Philippines and Sri Lanka. Four requests to transfer a total of $81 million to entities in the Philippines went through, but a request to transfer $20 million to a non-profit "foundation" in Sri Lanka raised suspicions because foundation's name was spelled incorrectly.

The transfers were suspended and the fraud was uncovered when the Bangladeshi bank was asked for clarification on the Sri Lankan transfer. By then $81 million had been transferred, primarily into accounts related to casinos in the Philippines. One casino returned $15 million to Bangladesh, but the rest had disappeared. The methods used in this attack—in particular the in-depth knowledge of the SWIFT systems and the steps taken to cover tracks—evidence Lazarus' growing technical skills.

Our analysis of this attack found code sharing between the malware and other unique tools used by Lazarus in other attacks, including some in the financial sector. Additionally, some of the tools used in the attack are connected to Lazarus. We have also seen this malware deployed against banks in the Philippines and Vietnam.

WANNACRY RANSOMWARE

Though the WannaCry outbreak became a global story on May 12, 2017, our analysis has revealed that an almost identical version of the ransomware was used in a small number of targeted attacks in February, March, and April of the same year. The key difference between the earlier versions of WannaCry and the one that became a global event was the method of propagation—the early version used stolen credentials to move through infected networks, while the May 12 version included the ability to self-propagate (known as a "worm") that led to its rapid spread.

In fact, within hours of the first detection, the May 12 version disrupted Britain's National Health Service and Spanish telecom provider Telefonica. After a day, it had infected more than 230,000 computers in over 150 countries. At that point the infection rate plummeted, largely through good luck—a security researcher in the United Kingdom had unknowingly triggered a kill switch when he registered a domain name he found within the code of the ransomware. This prevented the worm from moving laterally, greatly slowing the spread of the infection, effectively halting the initial outbreak and preventing it from becoming a significant event in the United States. Still, over the course of 3 days (May 12–15), we blocked WannaCry more than 22 million times on more than 300,000 devices. We were able to prevent WannaCry infections because we had already implemented protections for the underlying vulnerability.

The May version of WannaCry was unique and dangerous because of how quickly it could spread. It was the first ransomware-as-a-worm that has had global impact; once on a system it propagated autonomously using the "Eternal Blue" vulnerability in the Windows Server Messaging Block (SMB) protocol. After gaining access to a computer, WannaCry installs a ransomware package that works in the same fashion as most modern crypto-ransomware: it finds and encrypts a range of files, then displays a "ransom note" demanding a payment in bitcoin (in this case, $300 the first week; $600 the second week).

WannaCry spread largely to unpatched computers. Though Microsoft released a patch for the SMB vulnerability for Windows 7 and newer operating systems in

March, unpatched systems and systems running XP or older operating systems were unprotected. After the WannaCry outbreak began, Microsoft released a patch for XP and earlier platforms.

The May version of WannaCry was very effective at infecting computers and encrypting the data on them, but it also contained flaws that prevented the authors from collecting their ransom. Specifically, the ransomware was not coded correctly to allow the attackers to collect bitcoin payment from thousands of victims. Interestingly, the authors quickly recognized their error and released a corrected version 13 hours after the outbreak began, but that version did not spread widely before the infection was largely halted.

Our analysis found numerous links between WannaCry and known Lazarus operations. The ransomware shares some code with previous malware used by Lazarus as well as some custom tools connected to the group. Additionally, we found three pieces of malware linked to Lazarus on the network of the target of the very first WannaCry attack in February, at least one of which was used in the Sony Pictures attacks.

SONY PICTURES ENTERTAINMENT

In 2014, Sony was preparing for the holiday release of "The Interview", a film depicting the fictional assassination of North Korean leader Kim Jong-un. On November 24, Sony experienced a cyber attack that disabled its information technology network, destroyed data, and stole emails that were then leaked to the public in an effort to embarrass company officials.

Individuals claiming to be the hackers then sent emails threatening "9/11-style" terrorist attacks on theaters scheduled to show the film, leading some theaters to cancel screenings and for Sony to cancel its wide-spread release. Much of the media and public attention revolved around the free speech implications of the attack, as well as the release of salacious emails between Hollywood executives and celebrities as well as the salaries paid to different movie stars. But from a cybersecurity standpoint, the "big" story of the attacks was the permanent destruction of computers and data—by one report, impacting as much as three quarters of the computers and servers at Sony Pictures headquarters. Many were damaged by "wiper" malware known as "Destover," a particularly destructive variant which erased all the data on the machines, damaging them beyond repair.[1] The attacks reportedly had cascading effects that went well beyond the computers themselves—hampering essential administrative functions like employee payroll, insurance, and contracts. The destructive element of the Sony attack is what sets it apart from most cyber attacks.

On December 19, the FBI and the Director of National Intelligence (DNI) attributed the cyber attacks to the North Korean government based on a number of factors, including technical analysis on the wiper malware which included similar codes, encryption algorithms, and deletion methods to previous attacks linked to the North Korean government. Further, the FBI observed significant overlap in the infrastructure used to conduct the Sony attack and previously known North Korean command and control infrastructure. Last, many of the tools and tactics used in the Sony attack had similarities to a cyber attack in March of 2013 against South Korean banks and media outlets, which was carried out by North Korea.[2]

CONCLUSION

Lazarus is an aggressive and increasingly sophisticated attack group that has a demonstrated willingness to disrupt networks, steal money, and destroy computers and data. They learn from their mistakes and move rapidly from target to target. Unlike other major attack groups which typically focus on one sector or even one industry, Lazarus has no shown such limitations. This means that all industries and sectors, and all governments, have to assume that Lazarus may target them, and must prepare accordingly. Symantec continues to monitor Lazarus' activities and will continue to share information with our government partners as well as publish reports of the activity we observe. Thank you for the opportunity to testify, and I would be happy to take any questions that you may have.

Mr. PERRY. The Chair thanks the gentleman.

Dr. Pry, the Chair now recognizes you for your opening statement.

---

[1] *https://www.symantec.com/connect/blog/collaborative-operation-blockbuster-lazarus.*
[2] FBI National Press Office, "Update on Sony Investigation," December 19, 2014 *https://www.fbi.gov/news/pressrel/press-releases/update-on-sony-investigation.*

STATEMENT OF PETER VINCENT PRY, CHIEF OF STAFF, COMMISSION TO ASSESS THE THREAT TO THE UNITED STATES FROM ELECTROMAGNETIC PULSE ATTACK

Mr. PRY. Thank you for the opportunity to be here today to talk to you about the threat from North Korea, and particularly, the threat from electromagnetic pulse, EMP, which would result from the high-altitude detonation of a nuclear weapon. You know, generating an EMP, which is, in effect, a super energetic radio wave, you might think of it, or super lightening that would destroy electronic systems, including electric grids and all the critical infrastructures that support life in this country and that depend upon them.

This threat has been described a couple of times in the beginning of this hearing as unlikely. I would recommend that we not use that term in reference to an EMP. Maybe a better word would be "unknown." I suspect people will continue to describe an EMP threat as unlikely right up until the day before North Korea actually attacks us, just like we did with the 9/11 attack that, the day before it happened, would have been regarded as highly unlikely.

What we do know is that North Korea has the capability to make an EMP attack right now, and does, right now, constitute an existential threat to the United States. They detonated a hydrogen bomb on September 2. The new estimated yield on it is 250 kilotons. That single weapon could put an EMP field down out over, not just the United States, but all of North America that would cause the collapse of electric grids, transportation, communications, all the life-sustaining critical infrastructures.

Now, it wouldn't be a temporary blackout either. You know, it would take—we might not never recover from it. You know, if we are not prepared to defend our electric grid now and put in place the measures, and if they were to strike us now when we are unprotected, millions of Americans would die. Look at what is happening in Puerto Rico now if you want to know what the consequences of an EMP attack would be. They have only been without electricity for a few weeks and many people are in fear of their lives, legitimately so. Imagine a Puerto Rico where there was no U.S. Government coming to the rescue, all right, and they were on their own for a year. You would have most of the population of that island perish, if we weren't there to come in and help them. That is what would happen to the United States in the event of a North Korean nuclear EMP attack, which they could do today, all right, and with a single weapon.

The intelligence community. The EMP Commission has been virtually alone, I think, in having a more accurate estimate of the threat from North Korea than the intelligence community has over these years. This summer should have been a humbling experience, you know, for those who want to dismiss or minimize the North Korean threats. Just 6 months ago, you know, many people were arguing that North Korea only had as few as 6, perhaps as many as 30 nuclear weapons. Now the intelligence community estimates that they have got 60 nuclear weapons. All right? They weren't thought to have ICBMs that were capable of reaching the United States; maybe Alaska and Hawaii. Now we estimate that they can reach all of the United States.

So the intelligence community hasn't had a good record on this. The EMP Commission though, on the other hand, has been right.

Two days after that H bomb test, North Korea also released the technical report accurately describing the way a super EMP weapon would work. We think they probably have that too, which would generate EMP fields even more powerful than that of the H bomb that they successfully tested.

When we think of nuclear weapons, in the United States we think, well, North Korea would never cross the nuclear line, because for us, that is a big, deep dark red line that we would very reluctantly cross. But the North Koreans don't think that way about EMP, nor does Russia or China or Iran. In their military doctrine, EMP is part of a cyber warfare, it is part of a combined armed cyber warfare campaign.

The likelihood of a nuclear EMP attack is exactly the same as the likelihood of getting in a war with North Korea. If we get in a war with them, where they feel their regime is at risk, they will use everything within their power, including a nuclear EMP attack, to prevail.

So how likely is a nuclear war with North Korea? It is not just up to us. It is also up to the North Koreans themselves, and they are entirely capable of miscalculation.

Now, last, I'd like to just point in terms of what should we be doing. We are going in exactly the wrong direction in terms of our preparations for EMP. Just 2 weeks ago, a senior official at the Department of Homeland Security described the EMP threat as theoretical and something that we needed to study a lot longer. That is basically the plan that the U.S. Government is on now. The Department of Energy, the Department of Homeland Security, and the National labs want to spend millions of dollars continuing to study the EMP threat way out to 2020 and beyond, when the EMP Commission has already spent 17 years studying the threat, has repeatedly told Congress this is a real threat here and now and we know how to protect against and it can be done cost-effectively. That is all true.

I hope that a project called the Louisiana Project that the EMP Commission started with the Department of Homeland Security under Secretary Kelly will survive the death of the EMP Commission. In this project, we have been working with the State of Louisiana to prove that you can protect a State electric grid very cost-effectively. I think people will be surprised, if it is allowed to go forward, at how little it would cost, and it would provide a paradigm for all the other States to follow.

Thank you so much for hearing me out.

[The prepared statement of Mr. Pry follows:]

PREPARED STATEMENT OF PETER VINCENT PRY

OCTOBER 12, 2017

During the Cold War, major efforts were undertaken by the Department of Defense to assure that the U.S. National command authority and U.S. strategic forces could survive and operate after an EMP attack. However, no major efforts were then thought necessary to protect critical National infrastructures, relying on nuclear deterrence to protect them. With the development of small nuclear arsenals and long-range missiles by new, radical U.S. adversaries, beginning with North Korea, the threat of a nuclear EMP attack against the United States becomes one of the few ways that such a country could inflict devastating damage to the United States. It is critical, therefore, that the U.S. National leadership address the EMP threat as a critical and existential issue, and give a high priority to assuring the leadership is engaged and the necessary steps are taken to protect the country from EMP.

By way of background, the Commission to Assess the Threat to the United States from Electromagnetic Pulse (EMP) Attack was established by Congress in 2001 to advise the Congress, the President, Department of Defense, and other departments and agencies of the U.S. Government on the nuclear EMP threat to military systems and civilian critical infrastructures. The EMP Commission was re-established in 2015 with its charter broadened to include natural EMP from solar storms, all man-made EMP threats, cyber attack, sabotage, and Combined-Arms Cyber Warfare. The EMP Commission charter gives it access to all relevant Classified and Unclassified data and the power to levy analysis upon the Department of Defense.

On September 30, 2017, the Department of Defense, after withholding a significant part of the monies allocated by Congress to support the work of the EMP Commission for the entirety of 2016, terminated funding the EMP Commission. In the same month, North Korea detonated an H-Bomb that it plausibly describes as capable of "super-powerful EMP" attack and released a technical report "The EMP Might of Nuclear Weapons" accurately describing what Russia and China call a "Super-EMP" weapon.

Neither the Department of Defense nor the Department of Homeland Security has asked Congress to continue the EMP Commission. The House version of the National Defense Authorization Act includes a provision that would replace the existing EMP Commission with new Commissioners. Yet the existing EMP Commission comprises the Nation's foremost experts who have been officially or unofficially continuously engaged trying to advance National EMP preparedness for 17 years.

And today, as the EMP Commission has long warned, the Nation faces a potentially imminent and existential threat of nuclear EMP attack from North Korea. Recent events have proven the EMP Commission's critics wrong about other highly important aspects of the nuclear missile threat from North Korea:

- Just 6 months ago, most experts thought North Korea's nuclear arsenal was primitive, some academics claiming it had as few as 6 A-Bombs. Now the intelligence community reportedly estimates North Korea has 60 nuclear weapons.
- Just 6 months ago, most experts thought North Korea's ICBMs were fake, or if real could not strike the U.S. mainland. Now the intelligence community reportedly estimates North Korea's ICBMs can strike Denver and Chicago, and perhaps the entire United States.
- Just 6 months ago, most experts thought North Korea was many years away from an H-Bomb. Now it appears North Korea has H-Bombs comparable to sophisticated U.S. two-stage thermonuclear weapons.
- Just 6 months ago, most experts claimed North Korean ICBMs could not miniaturize an A-Bomb or design a reentry vehicle for missile delivery. Now the intelligence community reportedly assesses North Korea has miniaturized nuclear weapons, and has developed reentry vehicles for missile delivery, including by ICBMs that can strike the United States.[1]

After massive intelligence failures grossly underestimating North Korea's long-range missile capabilities, number of nuclear weapons, warhead miniaturization, and proximity to an H-Bomb, the biggest North Korean threat to the United States remains unacknowledged—nuclear EMP attack.

North Korea confirmed the EMP Commission's assessment by testing an H-Bomb that could make a devastating EMP attack, and in its official public statement: "The H-Bomb, the explosive power of which is adjustable from tens of kilotons to hundreds of kilotons, is a multi-functional thermonuclear weapon with great destructive power which can be detonated even at high altitudes for super-powerful EMP attack according to strategic goals."[2]

As noted earlier, Pyongyang also released a technical report accurately describing a "Super-EMP" weapon.[3]

---

[1] Joby Warwick, Ellen Nakashima, Anna Fifield, "North Korea Is No Making Missile-Ready Nuclear Weapons, U.S. Analysts Say" *Washington Post*, August 18, 2017; Michelle Ye Hee Lee, "North Korean Nuclear Test May Have Been Twice As Strong As First Thought" *Washington Post*, September 13, 2017; Jack Kim, Soyoung Kim, "North Korea Says It Has Developed A More Advanced Hydrogen Bomb That Can Be Loaded Onto An ICBM" *Business Insider,* September 2, 2017; *NBC News*, "'A Big Hoax': Experts Say North Korea Showing Off Missiles That Can't Fly" August 15, 2013.

[2] Bill Gertz, "Korea Nuclear Test Furthers EMP Bomb" *Washington Free Beacon*, September 6, 2017.

[3] Ibid. Kim Song-won, Dean of Kim Chaek University of Technology "The EMP Might of Nuclear Weapons" Rodong Sinmun, Pyongyang, September 4, 2017.

Just 6 months ago, some academics dismissed EMP Commission warnings and even, literally, laughed on National Public Radio at the idea North Korea could make an EMP attack.

PRIMITIVE AND "SUPER-EMP" NUCLEAR WEAPONS ARE BOTH EMP THREATS

The EMP Commission finds that even primitive, low-yield nuclear weapons are such a significant EMP threat that rogue states, like North Korea, or terrorists may well prefer using a nuclear weapon for EMP attack, instead of destroying a city: "Therefore, terrorists or state actors that possess relatively unsophisticated missiles armed with nuclear weapons may well calculate that, instead of destroying a city or military base, they may obtain the greatest political-military utility from one or a few such weapons by using them—or threatening their use—in an EMP attack."[4]

The EMP Commission 2004 Report warns: "Certain types of relatively low-yield nuclear weapons can be employed to generate potentially catastrophic EMP effects over wide geographic areas, and designs for variants of such weapons may have been illicitly trafficked for a quarter-century."[5]

In 2004, two Russian generals, both EMP experts, warned the EMP Commission that the design for Russia's Super-EMP warhead, capable of generating high-intensity EMP fields over 100,000 volts per meter, was "accidentally" transferred to North Korea. They also said that due to "brain drain," Russian scientists were in North Korea, as were Chinese and Pakistani scientists according to the Russians, helping with the North's missile and nuclear weapon programs. In 2009, South Korean military intelligence told their press that Russian scientists are in North Korea helping develop an EMP nuclear weapon. In 2013, a Chinese military commentator stated North Korea has Super-EMP nuclear weapons.[6]

Super-EMP weapons are low-yield and designed to produce not a big kinetic explosion, but rather a high level of gamma rays, which generates the high-frequency E1 EMP that is most damaging to the broadest range of electronics. North Korean nuclear tests, including the first in 2006, whose occurrence was predicted to the EMP Commission 2 years in advance by the two Russian EMP experts, mostly have yields consistent with the size of a Super-EMP weapon. The Russian generals' accurate prediction about when North Korea would perform its first nuclear test, and of a yield consistent with a Super-EMP weapon, indicates their warning about a North Korean Super-EMP weapon should be taken very seriously.

EMP THREAT FROM SATELLITES

While most analysts are fixated on when in the future North Korea will develop highly reliable intercontinental missiles, guidance systems, and reentry vehicles capable of striking a U.S. city, the threat here and now from EMP is largely ignored. EMP attack does not require an accurate guidance system because the area of effect, having a radius of hundreds or thousands of kilometers, is so large. No reentry vehicle is needed because the warhead is detonated at high-altitude, above the atmosphere. Missile reliability matters little because only one missile has to work to make an EMP attack against an entire Nation.

North Korea could make an EMP attack against the United States by launching a short-range missile off a freighter or submarine or by lofting a warhead to 30 kilometers burst height by balloon. While such lower-altitude EMP attacks would not cover the whole U.S. mainland, as would an attack at higher-altitude (300 kilometers), even a balloon-lofted warhead detonated at 30 kilometers altitude could blackout the Eastern Electric Power Grid that supports most of the population and generates 75 percent of U.S. electricity.

Or an EMP attack might be made by a North Korean satellite, right now.

A Super-EMP weapon could be relatively small and lightweight, and could fit inside North Korea's Kwangmyongsong–3 (KMS–3) and Kwangmyongsong–4 (KMS–4) satellites. These two satellites presently orbit over the United States, and over every other nation on Earth—demonstrating, or posing, a potential EMP threat against the entire world.

---

[4] Commission to Assess the Threat to the United States from Electromagnetic Pulse (EMP) Attack, *Executive Report*, 2004, p. 2.

[5] Ibid.

[6] U.S. Senate, Hearing, Statement for the Record, Dr. Peter Vincent Pry, "Foreign Views of Electromagnetic Pulse (EMP) Attack" testimony on behalf of EMP Commission before the Subcommittee on Terrorism, Technology, and Homeland Security, Senate Committee on the Judiciary (Washington, DC: March 9, 2005); Kim Min-sek and Yoo Jee-ho, "Military Source Warns of North's EMP Bomb" *JoonAng Daily* (September 2, 2009); Li Daguang, "North Korean Electromagnetic Attack Threatens South Korea's Information Warfare Capabilities" Tzu Chin, No. 260 (June 1, 2012) pp. 44–45.

North Korea's KMS–3 and KMS–4 satellites were launched to the south on polar trajectories and passed over the United States on their first orbit. Pyongyang launched KMS–4 on February 7, 2017, shortly after its fourth illegal nuclear test on January 6, that began the present protracted nuclear crisis with North Korea.

The south polar trajectory of KMS–3 and KMS–4 evades U.S. Ballistic Missile Early Warning Radars and National Missile Defenses, resembling a Russian secret weapon developed during the cold war, called the Fractional Orbital Bombardment System (FOBS) that would have used a nuclear-armed satellite to make a surprise EMP attack on the United States.[7]

Ambassador Henry Cooper, former director of the U.S. Strategic Defense Initiative, and a preeminent expert on missile defenses and space weapons, has written numerous articles warning about the potential North Korean EMP threat from their satellites. For example, on September 20, 2016 Ambassador Cooper wrote:

U.S. ballistic missile defense (BMD) interceptors are designed to intercept a few North Korean ICBMs that approach the United States over the North Polar region. But current U.S. BMD systems are not arranged to defend against even a single ICBM that approaches the United States from over the South Polar region, which is the direction toward which North Korea launches its satellites . . . This is not a new idea. The Soviets pioneered and tested just such a specific capability decades ago—we call it a Fractional Orbital Bombardment System (FOBS) . . . So, North Korea doesn't need an ICBM to create this existential threat. It could use its demonstrated satellite launcher to carry a nuclear weapon over the South Polar region and detonate it . . . over the United States to create a high-altitude electromagnetic pulse (HEMP) . . . The result could be to shut down the U.S. electric power grid for an indefinite period, leading to the death within a year of up to 90 percent of all Americans—as the EMP Commission testified over 8 years ago.[8]

Former NASA rocket scientist James Oberg visited North Korea's Sohae space launch base, witnessed elaborate measures undertaken to conceal space launch payloads, and concludes in a 2017 article that the EMP threat from North Korea's satellites should be taken seriously:

" . . . there have been fears expressed that North Korea might use a satellite to carry a small nuclear warhead into orbit and then detonate it over the United States for an EMP strike. These concerns seem extreme and require an astronomical scale of irrationality on the part of the regime. The most frightening aspect, I've come to realize, is that exactly such a scale of insanity is now evident in the rest of their 'space program.' That doomsday scenario, it now seems, has been plausible enough to compel the United States to take active measures to insure that no North Korean satellite, unless thoroughly inspected before launch, be allowed to reach orbit and ever overfly the United States."[9]

Kim Jong-un has threatened to reduce the United States to "ashes" with "nuclear thunderbolts" and threatened to retaliate for U.S. diplomatic and military pressure by "ordering officials and scientists to complete preparations for a satellite launch as soon as possible" amid "the enemies' harsh sanctions and moves to stifle" the North.[10] North Korean press (for example in Rodong Sinmun; March 7, 2016) asserts readiness for "any form of war" and includes their satellite with "strengthening of the nuclear deterrent and legitimate artificial satellite launch, which are our fair and square self-defensive choice." Moreover: "The nuclear [weapons] we possess are, precisely, the country's sovereignty, right to live, and dignity. Our satellite

---

[7] Miroslav Gyurosi, *The Soviet Fractional Orbital Bombardment System Program*, (January 2010) Technical Report APA–TR–2010–010.

[8] Ambassador Henry F. Cooper, "Whistling Past The Graveyard . . . " *High Frontier* (September 20, 2016) *highfrontier.org/sept-20-2016-whistling-past-the-graveyard/* See also: *highfrontier.org/category/fobs*. On up to 90 percent U.S. fatalities from an EMP attack, during a Congressional hearing, Rep. Roscoe Bartlett asked me if such high fatalities could result, and I responded: "We don't have experience with losing the infrastructure in a country with 300 million people, most of whom don't live in a way that provides for their own food and other needs. We can go back to an era when people did live like that. That would be—10 percent would be 30 million people, and that is probably the range where we could survive as a basically rural economy." U.S. House of Representatives, Hearing, "Threat Posed By Electromagnetic Pulse (EMP) Attack" Committee on Armed Services (Washington, DC: July 10, 2008), p. 9.

[9] Jim Oberg, *Space Review* (February 6, 2017) *www.thespacereview.com/article/3164/1* in a 2017 article.

[10] Alex Lockie, "North Korea Threatens 'Nuclear Thunderbolts' As U.S. And China Finally Work Together" *American Military News* (April 14, 2017); Fox News, "U.S. General: North Korea 'Will' Develop Nuclear Capabilities To Hit America" (September 20, 2016) *www.foxnews.com/world/2016/09/20/north-korea-says-successfully-ground-tests-new-rocket-engine.html*.

that cleaves through space is the proud sign that unfolds the future of the most powerful state in the world." The same article, like many others, warns North Korea makes "constant preparations so that we can fire the nuclear warheads, which have been deployed for actual warfare for the sake of national defense, at any moment!"

An earlier generation immediately understood the alarming strategic significance of Sputnik in 1957, yet few today understand or even care about the strategic significance of North Korea's satellites, perhaps because of wide-spread ignorance about EMP.

ADDRESSING MISINFORMATION

Misinformation about EMP abounds in the media, and even in many allegedly serious studies, from uninformed persons posturing as experts, who have no competency in EMP. False claims are often made that the EMP threat is "not real" but merely theoretical and greatly overblown.[11]

For example, one academic often quoted by the press claims that during the 1962 STARFISH PRIME high-altitude nuclear test, "just one string of street lights failed in Honolulu" and that this proved EMP is no threat.[12] In fact, the EMP knocked-out 36 strings of street lights, caused a telecommunications microwave relay station to fail, burned out HF (High-Frequency) radio links (used for long-distance communications), set off burglar alarms, and caused other damage.[13]

The Hawaiian Islands did not experience a catastrophic protracted blackout because they were on the far edge of the EMP field contour, where effects are weakest; are surrounded by an ocean, which mitigates EMP effects; and were still in an age dominated by vacuum tube electronics.

STARFISH PRIME was not the only test of this kind. Russia in 1961–62 also conducted a series of high-altitude nuclear bursts to test EMP effects over Kazakhstan, an industrialized area nearly as large as Western Europe.[14] That test destroyed the Kazakh electric grid.[15] Moreover, modern electronics, in part because they are designed to operate at much lower voltages, are much more vulnerable to EMP than the electronics of 1962 exposed to STARFISH PRIME and the Kazakh nuclear tests. A similar EMP event over the United States today would be an existential threat.[16]

Another academic wrongly asserts that because EMP from atmospheric nuclear tests in Nevada did not blackout Las Vegas, therefore EMP is no threat. The nuclear tests he describes were all endo-atmospheric tests that do not generate appreciable EMP fields beyond a range of about 5 miles. The high-altitude EMP (HEMP) threat of interest requires exo-atmospheric detonation, at 30 kilometers altitude or above, and produces EMP out to ranges of hundreds to thousands of miles. Las Vegas was not affected by the Nevada tests because they were endo-atmospheric nuclear tests that generated no HEMP.[17]

The same academic also miscalculates that "a 20-kiloton bomb detonated at optimum height would have a maximum EMP damage distance of 20 kilometers" in part, because he assumes "15,000 volts/meter or higher" in the E1 EMP component is necessary for damage. This figure is an extreme overestimate of system damage field thresholds. Damage and upset to electronic systems will happen from E1 EMP field strengths far below the academic's "15,000 volts/meter or higher." A one meter wire connected to a semiconductor device, such as a mouse cord or interconnection cable, would place hundreds to thousands of volts on microelectronic devices out to ranges of hundreds of miles for low-yield nuclear devices. Based on omission and

---

[11] See for example: Jeffrey Lewis, "Would A North Korean Space Nuke Really Lay Waste to the U.S.?" *New Scientist, www.newscientist.com/article/2129618*; Lewis quoted in Cheyenne MacDonald, "A North Korean 'Space Nuke' Wouldn't Lay Waste To America" *Daily Mail,* May 3, 2017; Lewis interviewed by National Public Radio, "The North Korean Electromagnetic Pulse Threat, Or Lack Thereof" *www.npr.org/2017/04/27/525833275; www.naturalnews.com/2017-05-01-npr-laughs-hysterically-north-korean-emp-nuclear-attack.html.*

[12] Ibid.

[13] Dr. William R. Graham, "North Korean Nuclear EMP Attack: An Existential Threat" 38 North, June 2, 2017.

[14] High-altitude EMP (HEMP), the phenomenon under discussion, results from the detonation of a nuclear weapon at high-altitude, 30 kilometers or higher. All nuclear weapons, even a primitive Hiroshima-type A-bomb, can produce levels of HEMP damaging to modern electronics over large geographic regions.

[15] According to Electric Infrastructure Security Council, Report: *USSR Nuclear EMP Upper Atmosphere Kazakhstan Test 184, (www.eiscouncil.org/APP_Data/upload/a4ce4b06-1a77-44d-83eb-842bb2a56fc6.pdf),* citing research by Oak Ridge National Laboratory, a comparable EMP event over the United States today "would likely damage about 365 large transformers in the U.S. power grid, leaving about 40 percent of the U.S. population without electrical power for 4 to 10 years."

[16] EMP Commission Executive Report, op. cit., pp. 4–8.

[17] Jack Liu, "A North Korean EMP Attack? . . . Unlikely" 38 North, May 5, 2017.

other experience with many EMP tests, semiconductor junctions, operating at a few volts, will experience breakdown at a few volts over their operating point, allowing their power supply to destroy the junctions experiencing breakdown.[18]

The same academic and many other non-experts also ignore system upset as a vulnerability. Digital electronics can be upset by extraneous pulses of a few volts. For unmanned control systems present within the electric power grids, long-haul communication repeater stations, and gas pipelines, an electronic upset is tantamount to permanent damage. Temporary upset of electronics can also have catastrophic consequences for military operations. No electronics should be considered invulnerable to EMP unless hardened and tested to certify survivability. Some highly critical unprotected electronics have been upset or damaged in simulated EMP tests, not at "15,000 volts/meter or higher," but at threat levels far below 1,000 volts/meter.[19]

The North Korean missile test on April 29, 2017, which apparently detonated at an altitude of 72 kilometers, the optimum height-of-burst for EMP attack by a 10 KT warhead, would create a potentially damaging EMP field spanning, not the academic's miscalculated 20 kilometers radius, but to about 930 kilometers radius [Kilometers Radius=110 (Kilometers Burst Height to the 0.5 Power)].[20]

Therefore, even for a low-yield 10–20 kiloton weapon, the EMP field should be considered dangerous for unprotected U.S. systems. The EMP Commission 2004 Report warned against the U.S. military's increasing use of commercial-off-the-shelf-technology that is not protected against EMP: "Our increasing dependence on advanced electronics systems results in the potential for an increased EMP vulnerability of our technologically advanced forces, and if unaddressed makes EMP employment by an adversary an attractive asymmetric option."[21]

EMPIRICAL BASIS FOR EMP THREAT BETTER ESTABLISHED THAN CYBER THREAT

The empirical basis for the threat of an EMP attack to electric grids and other critical infrastructures is far deeper and broader than the data for cyber attacks or sabotage. The notion that a cyber attack or sabotage can plunge the United States into a protracted blackout—while very real threats that warrant deep concern—are far more theoretical constructs than EMP attack.

We know for certain that EMP will cause wide-spread damage of electronics and protracted black-out of unprotected electric grids and other critical infrastructures from such hard data as:

- The U.S. STARFISH PRIME high-altitude nuclear test in 1962 over Johnston Island that generated an EMP field over the Hawaiian Islands, over 1,300 kilometers away, causing wide-spread damage to electronic systems.[22]
- Six Russian EMP tests 1961–1962 over Kazakhstan that with a single weapon destroyed electric grids over an area larger than Western Europe, proving this capability six times.[23]
- 30 years (1962–1992) of U.S. underground nuclear testing that included collecting data on EMP effects.
- Over 50 years of testing by EMP simulators, still on-going, including by the Congressional EMP Commission (2001–2008) that proved modern electronics are over 1 million times more vulnerable to EMP than the electronics of 1962.[24]

Moreover, hard data proving the threat from nuclear EMP is available from natural EMP generated by geomagnetic storms, accidental damage caused by electromagnetic transients, and non-nuclear radiofrequency weapons (RF weapons). All of these produce field strengths much less powerful than nuclear EMP, and in the case of accidental electromagnetic transients and radiofrequency weapons, much more localized. There are many thousands of such cases.

---

[18] Ibid.

[19] Ibid.

[20] Ibid.

[21] EMP Commission, *Executive Report*, op. cit., p. 47.

[22] Phil Plait, "The 50th Anniversary of Starfish Prime: The Nuke That Shook The World" *Discover*, July 9, 2012.

[23] Jerry Emanuelson, "Soviet Test 184: The 1962 Soviet Nuclear EMP Tests Over Kazakhstan" *Future Science*, Undated; Vladimir M. Loborev, "Up-to-Date State of the NEMP Problems and Topical Research Directions" Electromagnetic Environments and Consequences: Proceedings of the European International Symposium on Electromagnetic Environments, EUROEM Conference, Bordeaux, France, 1994; V. N. Mikhailov, *The Nuclear Tests of the USSR, Vol. 2*, Institute of Strategic Stability, Rosatom.

[24] "Electromagnetic Pulse: Threat to Critical Infrastructures" Hearing before the Subcommittee on Cybersecurity, Infrastructure Protection, and Security Technologies, House Committee on Homeland Security, Washington, DC: May 8, 2014.

Many documented examples of successful attacks using RF weapons, and accidents involving electromagnetic transients, are described in the Department of Defense *Pocket Guide for Security Procedures and Protocols for Mitigating Radio Frequency Threats* (Technical Support Working Group, Directed Energy Technical Office, Dahlgren Naval Surface Warfare Center). A few examples:

- "Radio Frequency Weapons were used in separate incidents against the U.S. Embassy in Moscow to falsely set off alarms and to induce a fire in a sensitive area."
- "In Kzlyar, Dagestan, Russia, Chechen rebel commander Salman Raduyev disabled police radio communications using RF transmitters during a raid."
- "In June 1999 in Bellingham, Washington, RF energy from a radar induced a SCADA malfunction that caused a gas pipeline to rupture and explode."
- "In 1999, a Robinson R–44 news helicopter nearly crashed when it flew by a high-frequency broadcast antenna."
- North Korea used a Radio Frequency Weapon, purchased from Russia, to attack airliners and impose an "electromagnetic blockade" on air traffic to Seoul, South Korea's capital. The repeated attacks by RFW also disrupted communications and the operation of automobiles in several South Korean cities in December 2010; March 9, 2011; and April–May 2012.[25]

VULNERABILITIES TO EMP

When assessing the potential vulnerability of U.S. military forces and civilian critical infrastructures to EMP, it is necessary to be mindful of the complex interdependencies of these highly networked systems, because EMP upset and damage of a very small fraction of the total system can cause total system failure.[26]

Real-world failures of electric grids from various causes indicate that a nuclear EMP attack would have catastrophic consequences. Significant and highly disruptive blackouts have been caused by single-point failures cascading into system-wide failures, originating from damage comprising far less than 1 percent of the total system. For example:

- The Great Northeast Blackout of 2003—that put 50 million people in the dark for a day, contributed to at least 11 deaths, and cost an estimated $6 billion—originated from a single failure point when a power line contacted a tree branch, damaging less than 0.0000001 (0.00001 percent) of the system.
- The New York City Blackout of 1977, that resulted in the arrest of 4,500 looters and injury of 550 police officers, was caused by a lightning strike on a substation that tripped two circuit breakers.
- The Great Northeast Blackout of 1965, that affected 30 million people, happened because a protective relay on a transmission line was improperly set.
- India's nation-wide blackout of July 30–31, 2012—the largest blackout in history, affecting 670 million people, 9 percent of the world population—was caused by overload of a single high-voltage power line.
- India's blackout of January 2, 2001—affecting 226 million people—was caused by equipment failure at the Uttar Pradesh substation.
- Indonesia's blackout of August 18, 2005—affecting 100 million people—was caused by overload of a high-voltage power line.
- Brazil's blackout of March 11, 1999—affecting 97 million people—was caused by a lightning strike on an EHV transformer substation.
- Italy's blackout of September 28, 2003—affecting 55 million people—was caused by overload of two high-voltage power lines.
- Germany, France, Italy, and Spain experienced partial blackouts on November 4, 2006—affecting 10–15 million people—from accidental shutdown of a high-voltage power line.
- The San Francisco blackout in April 2017 was caused by the failure of a single high-voltage breaker.

In contrast to the above blackouts caused by single-point or small-scale failures, a nuclear EMP attack would inflict massive wide-spread damage to the electric grid causing millions of failure points. With few exceptions, the U.S. National electric grid is unhardened and untested against nuclear EMP attack.

In the event of a nuclear EMP attack on the United States, a wide-spread protracted blackout is inevitable. This common-sense assessment is also supported by the Nation's best computer modeling:

---

[25] "Massive GPS Jamming Attack By North Korea" GPSWORLD.COM, May 8, 2012.

[26] Report of the Commission to Assess the Threat to the United States from Electromagnetic Pulse (EMP) Attack, *Critical National Infrastructures*, 2008, passim.

- Modeling by the U.S. Federal Energy Regulatory Commission (FERC) reportedly assesses that a terrorist attack that destroys just 9 of 2,000 EHV transformers—merely 0.0045 (0.45 percent) of all EHV transformers in the U.S. National electric grid—would be catastrophic damage, causing a protracted Nationwide blackout.
- Modeling by the Congressional EMP Commission assesses that a terrorist nuclear EMP attack, using a primitive 10-kiloton nuclear weapon, could destroy dozens of EHV transformers, thousands of SCADAS and electronic systems, causing catastrophic collapse and protracted blackout of the U.S. Eastern Grid, putting at risk the lives of millions.[27]

Thus, even if North Korea has only primitive, low-yield nuclear weapons, and likewise if other States or terrorists acquire one or a few such weapons, and the capability to detonate them at 30 kilometers or higher-altitude over the United States, as the EMP Commission warned over a decade ago in its 2004 Report: "The damage level could be sufficient to be catastrophic to the Nation, and our current vulnerability invites attack."[28]

WHAT IS TO BE DONE?

We recommend establishing an Executive Agent—a Cabinet Secretary designated by the President—with the authority, accountability, and resources, to manage U.S. National infrastructure protection and defense against EMP and the other existential threats described above. Current institutional authorities and responsibilities—Government, industry, regulatory agencies—are fragmented, incomplete, and unable to protect and defend against foreign hostile EMP threats or solar super-storms.

We encourage the President to work with Congressional leaders to stand-up an ad hoc Joint Presidential-Congressional Commission, with its members charged with supporting the Nation's leadership and providing expertise, experience, and oversight to achieve, on an accelerated basis, the protection of critical National infrastructures. The U.S. Federal Energy Regulatory Commission (FERC) and North American Electric Reliability Corporation (NERC) have for nearly a decade been unable or unwilling to implement the EMP Commission's recommendations. A Presidential-Congressional Commission on Critical Infrastructure Protection could engage the Free World's preeminent experts on EMP and Combined-Arms Cyber Warfare to serve the entire Government in a manner akin to the Atomic Energy Commission of the 1947–74 period, advising the administration's actions to attain most quickly and most cost-effectively the protection essential to long-term National survival and well-being. The United States should not remain in our current state of fatal vulnerability to well-known natural and man-made threats.

We highly commend President Trump's new Executive Order "Strengthening the Cybersecurity of Federal Networks and Critical Infrastructure" signed on May 11, 2017. We strongly recommend that implementation of cybersecurity for the electric grid and other critical infrastructures include EMP protection, since all-out cyber warfare as planned by Russia, China, North Korea, and Iran includes nuclear EMP attack. However, current institutional arrangements for protecting and improving the reliability of the electric grids and other critical infrastructures through the United States. FERC and the NERC are not designed to address major National security threats to the electric power grids and other National critical infrastructures. Using FERC and NERC to achieve this level of National security is beyond the purpose for which those organizations were created and has proven to be fundamentally unworkable. New institutional arrangements are needed to advance preparedness to survive EMP and related threats to our critical National infrastructures.

We recommend that U.S. military forces and critical National infrastructures be protected from EMP as outlined in the EMP Commission's Classified reports and Unclassified reports provided in 2004 and 2008. EMP protection of military systems and civilian/military critical National infrastructures can be achieved cost-effectively by a combination of operational procedures and physical hardening. It is not nec-

---

[27] For the best Unclassified modeling assessment of likely damage to the U.S. National electric grid from nuclear EMP attack see: U.S. Federal Energy Regulatory Commission (FERC) Interagency Report, coordinated with the Department of Defense and Oak Ridge National Laboratory: *Electromagnetic Pulse: Effects on the U.S. Power Grid, Executive Summary* (2010); FERC Interagency Report by Edward Savage, James Gilbert and William Radasky, *The Early Time (E1) High-Altitude Electromagnetic Pulse (HEMP) and Its Impact on the U.S. Power Grid* (Meta–R–320) Metatech Corporation (January 2010); FERC Interagency Report by James Gilbert, John Kappenman, William Radasky, and Edward Savage, *The Late-Time (E3) High-Altitude Electromagnetic Pulse (HEMP) and Its Impact on the U.S. Power Grid* (Meta–R–321) Metatech Corporation (January 2010).

[28] EMP Commission *Executive Report*, op. cit., p. 1.

essary to harden everything. Selective hardening of key critical nodes and equipment will suffice. Threat parameters are 200 kilovolts/meter for E1 EMP and 85 volts/kilometer for E3 EMP. Critical National infrastructures are already adequately protected from E2 EMP, equivalent to lightning.

We recommend, given the proximity and enormity of the threat from EMP and Combined-Arms Cyber Warfare, the President exercise leadership to implement immediate, mid-term, and long-term steps to deter and defeat this existential threat:

Immediately:

We recommend that the President declare that EMP or cyber attacks that black out or threaten to black out the National electric grid constitute the use of weapons of mass destruction that justify preemptive and retaliatory responses by the United States using all possible means, including nuclear weapons. Some potential adversaries have the capability to produce a protracted Nation-wide blackout induced by EMP or Combined-Arms Cyber Warfare by the use of nuclear or non-nuclear means. A Defense Science Board study *Resilient Military Systems and the Advanced Cyber Threat* (January 2013) equates an all-out cyber-attack on the United States with the consequences of a nuclear attack, and concludes that a nuclear response is justified to deter or retaliate for cyber warfare that threatens the life of the Nation: "While the manifestation of a nuclear and cyber attack are very different, in the end, the existential impact to the United States is the same."

We recommend that the President issue an Executive Order, provided to the previous White House, titled "Protecting the United States from Electromagnetic Pulse (EMP)". Among many other provisions to protect the Nation from EMP on an emergency basis, the Executive Order would instantly mobilize a much-needed "whole-of-Government solution" to the EMP and combined-arms cyber threat: "All U.S. Government Departments, Agencies, Offices, Councils, Boards, Commissions and other U.S. Government entities . . . shall take full and complete account of the EMP threat in forming policies and plans to protect United States critical infrastructures . . . " Protecting the electric grids and other critical infrastructures from the worst threat—nuclear EMP attack—can, if carried out in a system-wide, integrated approach, help mitigate all lesser threats, including natural EMP, man-made non-nuclear EMP, cyber attack, physical sabotage, and severe terrestrial weather.

We recommend that the President direct the Secretary of Defense to include a Limited Nuclear Option for EMP attack among the U.S. nuclear strike plans, and immediately make targeting and fusing adjustments to some of the nuclear forces needed to implement a nuclear EMP attack capability.

We recommend that the President direct the Secretary of Defense to use National technical means to ascertain if there is a nuclear weapon aboard North Korea's KMS–3 or KMS–4 satellites that orbit over the United States. If either or both of these satellites are nuclear-armed, they should be intercepted and destroyed over a broad ocean area where an EMP resulting from salvage-fusing will do the least damage to humanity.

We recommend that the President direct the Secretary of Defense to post Aegis ships in the Gulf of Mexico and near the east and west coasts, to search for and be prepared to intercept missiles launched from freighters, submarines, or other platforms that might make a nuclear EMP attack on the United States. U.S. National Missile Defenses (NMD) are primarily located in Alaska and California and oriented for a missile attack coming at the United States from the north, and are not deployed to intercept a short-warning missile attack launched near the U.S. coasts.

We recommend that the President direct the Secretary of Homeland Security to harden the FirstNet emergency communications system against EMP.

We recommend that the President initiate training, evaluating, and "Red Teaming" efforts to protect the United States and in the event of an EMP attack to respond, and periodically report the results of these efforts to the Congress.

Mid-Term:

We recommend that the President direct the Secretary of Defense to deploy Aegis-ashore missile interceptors along the Gulf of Mexico coast to plug the hole in U.S. missile defenses. The United States has no Ballistic Missile Early Warning System radars or missile interceptors facing south, and is largely blind and defenseless from that direction, including to missiles launched from submarines or off ships, or from a nuclear-armed satellite orbiting on a south polar trajectory.

We recommend that the President direct the Secretary of Defense to develop a space-surveillance program to detect if any satellites orbited over the United States are nuclear-armed, and develop space-interception capabilities to defend against nuclear-armed satellites that might make an EMP attack.

We recommend that the President direct the Nuclear Regulatory Commission to launch a crash program to harden the over 100 nuclear power reactors and their spent fuel storage facilities against nuclear EMP attack. Nuclear power reactors typically only have enough emergency power to cool reactor cores and spent fuel rods for a few days, after which they would "go Fukushima" spreading radioactivity over much of the United States.

Long-Term:

We recommend that the President through his Executive Agent protect elements of the National electric grids, the keystone critical infrastructure upon which all other critical infrastructures depend. Priority should be given to elements that are difficult and time-consuming to replace. Such elements can be protected from EMP at very low cost relative to the costs of an EMP catastrophe, and paid for without Federal dollars by a slight increase in user electric rates. We recommend that a similar approach be taken to key elements of the National telecommunications infrastructure and other National critical infrastructures.

We recommend the development and deployment of enhanced-EMP nuclear weapons and other means to deter adversary attack on the United States. Enhanced-EMP nuclear weapons, called by the Russians Super-EMP weapons, can be developed without nuclear testing.

We recommend strengthening U.S. ballistic missile defenses—including deployment of space-based defenses considered by the Strategic Defense Initiative—and that these be designed and postured to also protect the United States from EMP attack.

Mr. PERRY. The Chair thanks the gentleman.

If you just hold, votes have just been called. I have got to try and figure out what we are going to do here quick.

All right, folks, this is what we are going to do. Since the votes have been called, I am going to defer my questions, because I am going to come back. I am going to go to Mr. Duncan, Mr. Correa, and then to the other side. Then when the time is up, I am going to leave. We are going to vote, and then at least you know I am going to come back. If Mr. Higgins or anybody from—Ms. Barragán or anybody else from the other side wants to come back or anybody else on our side, you will have that option. I hope you guys can indulge us and stick around, but this is how things work here.

So, with that, I will recognize Mr. Duncan.

Mr. DUNCAN. I thank the Chairman for that. I thank the panel for being here. It has been very informative.

Dr. Pry, I am going to skip North Korea for just a second. Because of your past experience with Russian arms treaty verification, could you just touch on how difficult it is in Iran, as a closed society and a closed government, for our arms treaty folks and the IAEA to actually do inspections there? Then I have got a follow-up question about EMPs. But I would love to get your take on that.

Mr. PRY. Iran has actually—practically told us that they are cheating on the Iran nuclear deal. There is a military textbook called *Passive Defense* that is, you know, a major textbook taught at their general staff academies, that describes, in admiring terms, Soviet successful cheating on arms control treaties during the Cold War, and how they manage to fool us in terms of the number of weapons, the quality of their weapons, and that this would be a good paradigm to follow for Iran. I mean, it is there in black and white. Congressman Trent Franks has a copy of the book. Unfortunately, it is not Unclassified. It should be Unclassified, but it is For Official Use Only, and so it can only be used by, you know, U.S. Government officials.

But in effect, they have told us in their military doctrine black and white, you know, that they plan to cheat on agreements in order to get nuclear weapons.

In terms of the difficulty, I mean, I have written a number of articles on this. You know, at one of these military bases, there is a photograph that is actually available from Unclassified satellite imagery that shows four high-energy power lines, each one carrying about 750,000 volts, going down underground into a facility. Something is going on in one of those underground military facilities that require——

Mr. DUNCAN. These are at the military installation?

Mr. PRY. Yes, that the IAEA has never looked at, that they don't have an ability to investigate them. You know, that requires millions of volts of electricity. You know, that could be running uranium centrifuges that they have that have not been declared that could be running, something like the Krasnoyarsk–26. You asked about our Cold War experience. For example, the Soviet Union had a whole nuclear reactor secretly hidden underground at a place called Krasnoyarsk–26 so that they could cheat on arms control treaties and make plutonium and uranium for nuclear weapons, and tritium as well, you know, and cheat on the treaties.

Something that needs to be declassified is the—under President Reagan there was a thing called the General Advisory Committee Report on Arms Control Compliance 1959—I think it was 1983–84, up to that point, which the State Department has never allowed to be declassified. It goes through all of the major arms control treaties we had with the Soviet Union, demonstrate how they cheated on virtually every one.

So we have a long history of the bad guys cheating on these treaties. At least half the problem is our unwillingness to acknowledge that, you know, because there are interests in this town that are very much in favor of not wanting to face the reality that arms control doesn't work. Just like there were people, oh, around Neville Chamberlain before World War II that didn't want to acknowledge that the Nazis and the Japanese were cheating on the Washington Naval Treaty and other arms control agreements that existed before World War II.

Mr. DUNCAN. Thank you for that.

Thank you, Mr. Chairman.

Mr. PERRY. The Chair thanks the gentleman and the witness for their indulgence.

The Chair now recognizes the Ranking Member, Mr. Correa.

Mr. CORREA. Thank you, Mr. Chairman.

Mr. Ruggiero, very quickly, you talked about some of the things we can do, failed policies. The question to you and some of the others, have we ever gone after the bank accounts of North Korean generals, business folks? I mean, you hit them at the pocketbook at an individual level, that would get a reaction. Have we ever attempted to do that? Have we done that? If you lose a couple of billion dollars in a Swiss account, it may get your attention.

Mr. RUGGIERO. Certainly, that would be useful. I think on leadership funds there is a question of where that money is. I think you made a good recommendation there in terms of countries in Europe that have—bank secrecy is the best way to look at it.

In 2005, the United States went after Banco Delta Asia in Macao, which was very successful. But since that time, more recently, we have started to go after North Koreans. The issue here is that in a lot of ways, this money is held in China, in Chinese banks, or in the name of Chinese companies, and that is why it is important now to go after Chinese companies——

Mr. CORREA. So we haven't done—essentially, lack the technology, the information, the knowledge, to figure out how to get that money?

Mr. RUGGIERO. Well, I would say we are starting to do that now. Since May, the Trump administration has taken six actions against China.

Mr. CORREA. If I may interrupt you. Nuke testing 11 years ago, rocket testing 20 years ago. If you figure, they are preparing for that even before that and it is just barely now that we are figuring this out.

Mr. RUGGIERO. Certainly.

Mr. CORREA. Very quickly, Dr. Pry, you talked about an EMP pulse not being theoretical, but essentially, a clear and present situation. Why haven't we reacted to it as a country? Is this a question of politics or is this a question of cost? If the answer is this is a threat here, we are going to go have to invest a lot of money to harden our systems.

Mr. PRY. It isn't chiefly a question of cost. You can actually protect against EMP quite cost effectively. The EMP Commission estimated that for $2 billion, you know, we could protect the electric grid. You know, that is what we give away every year in foreign aid to Pakistan.

I think it is a complex question as to why we haven't acted yet. Politics is mostly what it has to do with.

The electric utilities in this country are not controlled by the Federal Government. You know, there are 3,000 independent utilities. No agency of the U.S. Government, including the U.S. Federal Energy Regulatory Commission, has the legisla-—has the authority, has the power to order them to protect the electric grid. They have spent vast amounts of money and huge effort lobbying against EMP, and not just EMP——

Mr. CORREA. But I would argue exactly that that is kind-of what we are going through with cybersecurity right now.

Mr. PRY. Exactly, exactly.

Mr. CORREA. Private sector, some folks want to step up, some folks don't. Even the Federal Government, some folks—you know, agencies are there, some are not.

Mr. PRY. The NERC has even opposed the tree branch threat. I mean, the great Northeast blackout of 2003 was caused when a tree branch hit a high-power voltage line in Ohio, and it put 50 million Americans in the dark. FERC begged them to come up with a plan to avoid the tree branch threat in the future, because we can't have 50 million Americans in the dark. It has taken them 10 years to come up with a better, improved——

Mr. CORREA. Thank you very much.

Mr. PERRY. The Chair thanks the gentleman.

The Chair now recognizes Mr. Higgins.

Mr. HIGGINS. Mr. Chairman, in the interest of time, I defer my questions till we return.

Mr. PERRY. Yes, sir.

The Chair now recognizes Miss Rice.

Miss RICE. Thank you, Mr. Chairman.

This, I guess, is a question I would put to any of you on the panel. What effect would President Trump's anticipated act to de-certify the Iran nuclear deal have on any potential diplomatic solution to the North Korea issue?

Mr. RUGGIERO. Well, I would just say that the North Koreans are not waiting by the phone to have a negotiated settlement. That would be the first. The second is that, from my perspective, it is the Iranians that are looking at North Korea and seeing their pathway to a nuclear weapon.

The concern I have is that there are many people who are suggesting we should stay in the Iran deal, that are the same people that are saying we can accept the threat from North Korea right now and just deter them. I think that is the wrong message to Iran. I think that we have to, when we are looking at North Korea, we have to make sure that we underscore that our policy is denuclearization, so that the Iranians don't see that, in 20 years, they have a path to a nuclear weapon.

Mr. PRY. If I could make a comment on this. You know, we have, this summer, been surprised by the advancement of the missile and nuclear weapons threat from North Korea. I think the next big surprise that is going to face us is Iran, because we have grossly underestimated the Iranian nuclear threat. If we want to read carefully the 2014 International Atomic Energy Agency report, while they did not come to the conclusion—the IAEA doesn't draw these conclusions, but members are our commission and former members of the Clinton and Reagan administration intelligence communities looked at that report. There are indicators, technological indicators, that Iran already has the bomb, and that they may have had the bomb since before 2003.

Before 2003, there were actually manufacturing bridge wire detonators, neutron initiators, and they had conducted an implosion experiment. In the Manhattan Project during World War II when the United States was at that technological phase, we were 3 months from getting the atomic bomb. Now, these were things they were doing before 2003. What is going on in those military facilities? Personally, I think they have already got the bomb, and that we are going to be surprised just like we have been about North Korea.

Miss RICE. Anyone else?

Okay. Thank you.

Mr. PERRY. The gentlelady yields.

The Chairman recognizes Ms. Barragán.

Ms. BARRAGÁN. While I am looking for my questions, I just want to do a quick follow-up to that. I have read a lot of people who have opined on the Iran deal, and a lot of folks who did not support the deal are still coming out very publicly and saying, even though this is not the best deal, the manner in which the President wants to do it is not the way to do it, and that is a risk.

Does anybody have any thoughts on the manner in which it is being done? I will just leave it at that.

Mr. PRY. I would like to volunteer my opinion on this. You know, I think the biggest risk is remaining in the deal. I see it in the press. I see it in the defenders of the Iran nuclear deal describing it that at least it has constrained the nuclear threat from Iran, that it has contained the nuclear threat from Iran. That is not a fact. There is no evidence that it is contained. Then there is plenty of evidence that it hasn't contained the threat from Iran and that we have basically deluded ourselves in this deal into thinking that we have contained a threat that actually——

Ms. BARRAGÁN. So I just want to respectfully—do you think the process in which the President is following is the right approach on this? Yes or no.

Mr. PRY. I think anything that gets—yes. Anything that gets us out of that deal is going to be in interest of our survival.

Ms. BARRAGÁN. Thank you.

Okay. So I want to go ahead and follow up on—just in the last 10 days, between attacking the press and the First Amendment and blaming Puerto Ricans for the disaster caused by Hurricane Maria, the President tweeted the following in regards to North Korea: Our country has been unsuccessfully dealing with North Korea for 25 years, giving billions of dollars and getting nothing. Policy didn't work.

Next tweet: Presidents and their administrations have been talking to North Korea for 25 years. Agreements made and massive amounts of money paid hasn't worked. Agreements violated before the ink was dry. Making fools of U.S. negotiators. Sorry, but only one thing will work.

The President's next tweet: Just heard foreign minister of North Korea speak at U.N. If he echoes thoughts of little rocket man, they won't be around much longer.

Last: We can't allow this dictatorship to threaten our Nation and our allies with unimaginable loss of life, he said at a meeting with top military officers.

Finally: We will do what we must to prevent that from happening, and it will be done if necessary, believe me.

Mr. Greene, how would you characterize this administration's North Korea strategy? What are the implications of the President's diplomacy by tweet foreign policy, especially considering the rift between the President and his Secretary of State, Rex Tillerson?

Mr. GREENE. So unfortune—so I am the cyber expert here, and unfortunately, I am not qualified to opine on the merits or lack thereof a diplomatic approach. So I apologize, I am not capable of responding on that.

Ms. BARRAGÁN. Does anybody on the panel believe that the President's diplomacy by tweeting is the proper way to go? That is a yes or no.

Mr. PRY. Yes.

Ms. BARRAGÁN. Okay. Mr. Ruggiero.

Mr. RUGGIERO. I think that is tougher to answer via yes, no. There is a lot in there in terms of North Korea policy. I think the President is right when he talks about diplomacy has not worked with North Korea. I think that——

Ms. BARRAGÁN. Don't you think there is a threat of us getting into a nuclear war because the President may tweet something to set off the other side?

Mr. RUGGIERO. Well, that was going to be my next point, which is, essentially, when you are talking about deterrence, it is important to telegraph to the other side what the consequence of an action will be. I think the United States and North Korea have done that, but on both sides it has gone too far. I think the evidence of miscalculation can happen.

Ms. BARRAGÁN. Thank you. I have one more question for Mr. Greene.

Mr. PERRY. Can the gentlelady yield until we come back? We have got a minute to vote. I apologize, but I want to adjourn the committee at this time—recess—correction—the committee at this time.

So a vote has been called on the House floor. The committee will recess until 10 minutes after the last vote.

[Recess.]

Mr. PERRY. Thank you all for your indulgence and your patience. The Subcommittee on Oversight and Management Efficiency will come to order. So the Chair will now recognize himself for 5 minutes of questioning. Just be apprised we are back to the 5-minute schedule since we don't have votes impending.

So let me see if I can get my head here in the game quickly. Mr. Cilluffo, 6,000 hackers employed in China and Southeast Asia. I want to talk to you about that a little bit and the indicators and the intelligence prep of the battlefield just to set your mind frame. So these hackers that are employed in China and Southeast Asia—and maybe I should also include Mr. Greene, because maybe this is some of this Lazarus—some of these Lazarus folks. I don't know. But do we—obviously, it is a little tougher for us to track these people in China. Do we track them at all? If not China, Southeast Asia seems like it would be a more opportune intelligence target for us. Do we track them? Do the host countries where they are operating know that they are there such that we could impose a sanction or some kind of financial penalty or some kind of penalty on that host country that is hosting these individuals? Is that a possibility?

Mr. CILLUFFO. Mr. Chairman, I think that is an excellent question.

To clarify, the 6,000 is not exclusively those operating overseas, but a vast majority or many of them actually do. But I do think you raise a great question here, and that is finding levers and points of leverage that we can have with other—including allies, by the way—where we can apply greater physical pressure in addition to cyber means. I mean, if you look at a photo, a satellite photo of the Koreas at night, I mean, South Korea is lit up like a Christmas tree; North Korea is dark. So there is very little connectivity there. So, obviously, when we look at some of our own capabilities and capacities, retaliation in kind is going to have minimal effect and impact because they don't have a whole lot to take down. So, when you start looking at these outposts that they do have, I think we do have opportunities to apply new means of pressure, and I do think that many of these countries are unwitting to some of these operatives. So I think that that is a path that should be pursued, and we should light them up.

Mr. PERRY. What about the indicators? When you say, you know, it is essentially IPB and that these are indicators, you talk about stand-alone, the broader campaign, and then indicators. For instance, keeping with Dr. Pry, if we are to be—and I think we should be—rightly concerned about EMP as a method—or any of the other things, but let's stick with EMP—for example, would there be specific indicators in cyber that would clue us into impending testing, utilization, et cetera?

Mr. CILLUFFO. You know, I think Dr. Pry rightfully framed the issue that, at the end of the day, it is not the modality; it is the question of whether or not they get into the game. If they get into the game, they will come in wholesale if they feel threatened. So I think that the indicators are significant in terms of potential target selection. But I am not necessarily sure there would be any specific to EMP, other than they are going after the grid pretty—so, if there is one critical infrastructure that every other critical infrastructure is dependent upon, all the life-line sectors, it is electric; it is the grid. They could come at that through cyber means or, obviously, catastrophically through EMP attacks.

Mr. PERRY. I can see we are going to go to round two, so I am going to try and limit my comments here. But, Mr. Greene, I am going to get to you. So just hang on there a little bit, but I want to stay with Mr. Cilluffo just for continuity here.

So you mentioned in your remarks the targeting of U.S. energy companies. Have they done that? Do we have the indicators that they have done—I mean, can we prove that at this point? That is known information to us?

Mr. CILLUFFO. This is now known information, yes. There have been actual reports put out by the information sharing and analysis centers for industrial control systems and for the energy sector in particular. There was a news report that just popped earlier this week specifically about a particular energy company that was breached. That is based on information that——

Mr. PERRY. It was breached by the North Koreans or we believe——

Mr. CILLUFFO. Allegedly that is what the attempt is. So I think that one thing to notify, to keep in mind, in addition to IPB—where it could signal targets, it could signal intentions—it is also worth noting: If you can exploit, you can also attack.

Mr. PERRY. Sure.

Mr. CILLUFFO. In other words, if you are in the system——

Mr. PERRY. Right.

Mr. CILLUFFO [continuing]. You are in the system. It all hinges around intentions, and if they have got a foothold in the system and their intention is to attack, they can also attack.

Mr. PERRY. All right. I am going to yield, and at this time, I will recognize the gentleman from Louisiana, Mr. Higgins.

Mr. HIGGINS. Thank you, Mr. Chairman.

Dr. Pry, my questions will be addressed at you, sir. So that you can get your head wrapped around where I am going with this, I am specifically going to be asking about North Korea's satellite program and their so-called space program and the KMS–4 satellite launch in February of this year.

I have read your entire testimony. It is fascinating, quite informative. You refer to massive intelligence failures grossly underestimated North Korea's long-range missile capabilities, the number of nuclear weapons, warhead miniaturization, the development of an H-bomb, et cetera. Do you stand by that statement, sir?

Mr. PRY. Oh, absolutely, as does Dr. Graham, the chairman of our commission.

Mr. HIGGINS. Moving on. In 2004, you stated that two Russian generals, both EMP experts, warned the EMP Commission that the design for Russia's super EMP warhead, capable of generating high-intensity EMP fields, was transferred to North Korea. Not long after that, in 2006, North Korea nuclear tests indicated yields that were consistent with the size of a super EMP weapon. The timing and indicators of that illegal nuclear test were reflective of the warnings as stated by the two Russian experts. Is that correct?

Mr. PRY. Yes, that is correct, sir.

Mr. HIGGINS. A super EMP weapon, according to your testimony, can be relatively small and lightweight and can fit inside North Korea's KMS–3 or KMS–4 satellites. These two satellites—specifically, I am referring to KMS–4, because it was launched this year—presently orbit the United States and over every other nation on Earth through the southern polar trajectory. The south polar trajectory evades U.S. ballistic missile early warning radars and National missile defenses, which also resembles a Russian secret weapon developed during the Cold War similar to a super EMP weapon. Is that correct?

Mr. PRY. Yes, that is correct.

Mr. HIGGINS. Two experts cited in your testimony stated similar concerns, one confirming that current ballistic missile defense systems are not arranged to defend against even a single ICBM or satellite that approaches the United States from the south polar region. Another expert stated that North Korea might use a satellite to carry a small nuclear warhead into orbit and then detonate it over the United States for an EMP strike.

Now, considering the fact that it appears that North Korea has had access to a design for a super EMP warhead for over a decade now, according to the Russian experts that were accurate in their predictions of North Korean nuclear tests 2 years later and the indicators of that test, that would suggest that it was a detonation of a super EMP device, would you concur that it is possible or even probable that KMS–4 is currently super EMP-armed?

Mr. PRY. We are very concerned about that. You know, we don't know if they are nuclear armed or not, but we know Kim Jong-un is a high-risk player, and we think the threat is intolerable to pose an existential threat to our society that passes over the country several times a day and have recommended that the satellites be shot down over a broad ocean area, over the arctic region, so that, just in case they are salvage-fused for EMP, you know, they would go off over an area that would limit the damage to humanity. But, yes, we are very concerned about that.

Mr. HIGGINS. Would you assess, sir, that the EMP threat is significant enough, that the existing EMP threat, specifically with regards to KMS–4, would you assess that that threat is significant enough to warrant legislation out of this body, as suggested through this subcommittee, mandating the hardening of our grid and the shielding of our grid, as you mentioned earlier in your testimony?

Mr. PRY. Well, absolutely. Sir, even before the North Koreans launched these satellites, back in 2008, that was the recommendation of the EMP Commission because we feared exactly this kind of development. There are two satellites currently in orbit, one that was launched in 2012. They may launch them in the future. What they appear to be trying to do is create a constellation so that they will, in the near term, always have a satellite in close proximity to North America. You know, if we don't act to defend ourselves and/or take out those satellites, you know, eventually, we will be in a situation where we can't easily take the satellites out without the United States being at risk.

Mr. HIGGINS. Thank you for your testimony.

Mr. Chairman, thank you for indulging my time, and I yield back.

Mr. PERRY. The Chairman thanks the gentleman, deviates from protocol and, in the interest of time, recognizes the Ranking Member, Mr. Correa, for the beginning of the second round.

Mr. CORREA. Thank you.

Question, Mr. Greene, in terms of cyber—North Korean cyber attack motivation undermining the United States, what is the higher probability, them going after our critical infrastructure or stealing intellectual property from us?

Mr. GREENE. So, with the Lazarus Group, which has been linked by the FBI to North Korea, it is hard to say because they have not shown any limitation to what they are willing to do. They have gone after critical infrastructure. They have gone after financial. They have gone after intellectual property.

The recent report that Mr. Cilluffo was talking about is concerning because it shows this probing of the battlefield, initial efforts to try to get their way into electric systems. We had a report—not Lazarus, it was a different actor—just a couple of weeks ago about compromises of control systems at energy facilities. Previously, we had seen this actor working on the back-end management systems. In the 2 years after that, they moved on to the control systems. So there clearly is an effort.

The group that was reported publicly this week has been consistent with the Lazarus Group. So to see them moving into the electric grid—and have public reporting on it—suggests to me a renewed interest there, which is worrisome. Depending upon what outcome they want, you are going to get a better geopolitical outcome by going after the grid than you are by going after intellectual property.

Mr. CORREA. So, following up on that train of thought, if you go after Sony, if you go after bank accounts, you may be doing it out of a hotel room in Japan or maybe somewhere in China or, now, based on the fact that the Russian state-owned company TransTelekom is now working with North Korea, I mean, you can have those kinds of thefts directly and indirectly. They are kind of a little vague in terms of who did it and where the smoking gun is. But if you go after our power grid and you shut it down, that is a little more direct of an attack. I mean, that is kind-of a declaration here.

Mr. GREENE. If you are trying to track back, technically, you are looking at who is doing it; it is going to be the same technical means to see where the attack is coming from. You rarely see the last hop to an attack actually come from the bad actor's computer. They are going to compromise someone else's computer. A lot of the attacks that happen in the United States that are based from overseas, the attacking computer is actually in the United States, but it is compromised. It is a bot. So, from that standpoint, it could come from anywhere.

Again, in terms of motivations, we have seen the Lazarus Group over the past couple years focus on financial gain. That temporally has coincided with when the sanctions have gotten worse. The ransomware WannaCry, there was some speculation as to whether they were really trying to get money out of WannaCry. There has been a fairly robust debate in the media circles that I spend my days in. But what we saw in WannaCry, it was originally miscoded to collect ransom. Within I believe it was 13 hours, they released a new version when they realized they weren't collecting ransom. So that suggests to me that that actually was an effort to get money. Again, that coincides with the increased new sanctions. The same thing with the attacks on the Bangladesh banks, the Polish bank heists. There has been an uptick in the effort to get money. But, at the same time, that was soon after the Sony attack.

So I guess what I am saying, perhaps unartfully, is that this group works on multiple different attacks, multiple different goals.

Mr. CORREA. Let me flip around the question and ask you: You have seen those coordinated attacks coming. Has our response world-wide been a coordinated defense just like it was when we got the ransomware just recently where most of the world kind-of reacted very quickly? Do we have that kind of a coordinated response to North Korea? Are they part of that, you know, folks that we are looking at to make sure they don't surprise us with these kinds of attacks?

Mr. GREENE. So, with respect to their main actor, the Lazarus Group, yeah, there is pretty good coordination, public-private partnership. The WannaCry response was probably the best public-private partnership I have ever seen. We were on the phone with DHS and the White House Friday night, throughout the weekend, connecting up our experts. They were sending us indicators of compromise for analysis. We were sending them back. So there is a growing ability to coordinate in cyber response. It is kind-of like the snowball going down the hill. Over the past 3 to——

Mr. CORREA. I would imagine the key to the coordinated cyber response is time. You have to do it almost instantly, within split seconds.

Mr. GREENE. Yeah. So, when I first heard reports of WannaCry, I confirmed with our experts that this was real. I shot out a couple emails to the White House, to DHS, and I got almost immediate responses. We had experts talking and exchanging in a matter of minutes. That was very strong.

The concern I would have is that still is somewhat relationship-based. We need to have that happening not because these are folks that I know or they know me; there has to be something more structured in place.

Mr. CORREA. Thank you, Mr. Chair.

Mr. PERRY. The Chair thanks the gentleman.

I am going to start the second round, which looks like it is going to be me. Are you leaving? You gotta go?

Mr. CORREA. No comment.

Mr. PERRY. Okay. All right. So it will just be us. We will have a good time together.

Let me just start with Mr. Cilluffo and kind-of finish where we were headed there. The targeting of the United States energy companies and indicators, do you know whether we are—we, the Federal Government, Homeland Security, and related agencies—are aware of the indicators and are monitoring the indicators developing that intelligence, so to speak?

Mr. CILLUFFO. You know, in general terms, Mr. Chairman, they are. We recently—the Federal Government recently stood up CTIIC, the Cyber Threat Integration and Intelligence Center, underneath the Office of the Director of National Intelligence, which is meant to provide the situational awareness of all the overseas intelligence we may have and kludging that and combining that with what we may have domestically.

Mr. PERRY. Who is collecting domestically?

Mr. CILLUFFO. So FBI would have different indicators, but the private sector, they are the owners and operators. They are the ones who have got better insights into their own critical infrastructures, into their data, and into particular breaches. So it really is— we talk public-private partnerships. I have been a little critical, saying "long on nouns, short on verbs." We have been talking about it forever, admiring the problem. But we are starting to see some genuine solution sets there. I think this gets to the bigger set of questions. I mean, at the end of the day, the private sector is on the front lines of this battle. Very few companies went into business thinking they have to defend themselves against foreign militaries or foreign intelligence services. It is an unlevel playing field. So how can the Federal Government provide information, but at the flip side, the private sector provides some of those solution sets too. So it is in where the two come together that the magic is.

Mr. PERRY. Do you have recommendations in that regard regarding a governmental—for the homeland, in particular, understanding that the intelligence services, and maybe DOD is handling foreign threats. But for threats in the homeland, I am a little uncomfortable, quite honestly, feel like we are laid a little bare there just counting on the private sector, which, with all due respect, they are focused on their business and trying to make a living, right?

Mr. CILLUFFO. Absolutely.

Mr. PERRY. So this isn't supposed to be their primary focus, but it seems like it should be one of ours.

Mr. CILLUFFO. You know, and I think you should have a specific tiger team set up to deal with the North Korean threat in particular, because we talk about cyber and cyber deterrence—you don't deter cyber. You deter actors from engaging in certain activity, whether nuclear, cyber, or otherwise. So I do think there is an opportunity to build a team here specifically.

Mr. PERRY. There is nothing currently that you know of?

Mr. CILLUFFO. I may be unaware. Hopefully, there is some activity inside the Federal Government. But is it as whole and wholesome as it needs to be? Probably not.

Mr. PERRY. Okay. Fair enough.

All right. Mr.—am I saying—is part of your name—I noticed Mr. Correa kind of kept some of it silent. Please tell me how you pronounce your name. I want to get it right.

Mr. RUGGIERO. Sure. Ruggiero.

Mr. PERRY. Ruggiero. Okay. Thank you.

All right. So you talked about the Department must be publishing a vessel list regarding North Korea—saying we think they have 40, but you are saying it is up to 140. It seems to me a bit odd. So it might be out of place. You can walk me through it. Is this the Department of Homeland's responsibility? Should it be their responsibility? Under what kind of authority, I guess?

Then I want to talk to you about this 180-day grace period regarding sanctions to get the list. So I am not sure I understand that fully. So if you can elaborate us on those two things.

Mr. RUGGIERO. Sure. In the sanctions law that was signed by the President, I believe in August, there are some authorities for the Department of Homeland Security probably would have to work with the Treasury Department in terms of vessel lists. The issue with North Korea now is it is easy to identify vessels that have the North Korea flag or the ones that visit North Korea. But they are very good at deceptive practices in the commercial and financial sphere where they use Chinese and Hong Kong and other front companies. We believe that that is some of what they are doing in the shipping sector, which makes it harder.

Mr. PERRY. Okay.

Mr. RUGGIERO. So that is where that delta comes from. That is why we use the phrase "at least." There are other lists that are much higher than that. So, I think, you know, this is an area—my experience comes also on the Iran side, where we targeted Iran's shipping sector, and it was very successful. That is an area now that we are not doing enough on North Korea, and I think Homeland Security could help with that. They have some authorities that could be used.

I think Treasury Department, State Department—and the point on the tiger team, we don't see that and the U.S. Government sort-of going at sanctions in this way. So I think there is some focus on it, but we need to have more.

Mr. PERRY. Okay. The 180 days, there is a prohibition or restriction regarding the sanctions regime?

Mr. RUGGIERO. That is the requirement when the Department of Homeland Security has to make some of these judgments in the law. So the point I was making is you can do it earlier than 180 days.

Mr. PERRY. Okay. Do we know—and keeping with you, sir, you mentioned in your testimony the sale of nuclear materials. I don't know if we are talking about equipment, et cetera, and also chemical. Do you have any examples of those that we need to be aware of that we are maybe not aware of at least on the committee?

Mr. RUGGIERO. Well, in terms of nuclear, the biggest case was in 2007 when Israel destroyed a nuclear reactor in Syria. There has been, you know, rumors that North Korea exchanged nuclear material with Libya in that same time frame.

On the chemical weapons side, I detail briefly in my testimony about the Syria connections, which are not linked to the more recent ones. But, you know, talking about chemical weapons, suits, and other items. I mean, these are relationships that are very strong between Syria and North Korea.

Mr. PERRY. So, at least there is a documented history, maybe it is not updated or maybe it is not current from a known fact standpoint, but that might just be because we don't know yet, we haven't found out?

Mr. RUGGIERO. My experience is, you know, as I said, North Korea will sell anything to anyone who is willing to pay.

Mr. PERRY. Sure.

Mr. RUGGIERO. You know, there was a time where we thought that nuclear was a line they were not willing to cross, and they proved that they are willing to do that.

Mr. PERRY. Okay. Excuse me just for one moment.

Mr. Terrell, I know you have been—you are almost exhausted with your participation here. Blister and nerve agents, and I think the world—at least I do—fundamentally believes that VX was used on Kim Jong-un's half-brother in Malaysia. You know, I have got a little bit of military experience as well. My chief of staff is a chemical officer. With that, those eventualities were very concerning to anybody that has any idea what they are seeing there.

Maybe the nerve—first, let me ask you this. I don't know what your background is. But I want to just get for the record, and I'd like to hear from you folks. Conventional artillery—conventional—so I think we have assessed that the North Koreans have as many as 10,000 conventional tubes pointed at the 25 million people living in Seoul, 60-plus or -minus miles away, right? Nerve and blister agents or chemical agents are deliverable by conventional artillery, are they not?

Mr. TERRELL. Yes, sir. They are deliverable by conventional artillery, rockets, and short-range ballistic missiles.

Mr. PERRY. Sure. Do you know and can you comment on whether conventional artillery, rockets, missiles, et cetera, all require electronics or electricity to operate?

Mr. TERRELL. Not all of their tube artillery would.

Mr. PERRY. Right. So that is just pulling the lanyard, right——

Mr. TERRELL. Pulling the lanyard.

Mr. PERRY [continuing]. Downrange. Right. So that is a concern there.

They have sufficient stockpiles, according to your testimony, or at least what I read. You didn't dispute.

Mr. TERRELL. South Korean ROK Minister of National Defense estimates between 2,500 and 5,000 metric tons.

Mr. PERRY. Right. Right. So that is certainly enough for a first round exchange, right?

Mr. TERRELL. Right.

Mr. PERRY. What about deliverable for a long distance? You have mentioned rocket or ballistic missiles. So this is literally something—let's just take VX. Deliverable by a ballistic missile over a large population or a large area?

Mr. TERRELL. So they could deliver VX or mustard blister agent by scuds. You know, most likely targets for those would be places like Busan——

Mr. PERRY. Right.

Mr. TERRELL [continuing]. Looking at stopping force flow into the theater.

Mr. PERRY. But we are not talking about—so, in your opinion, we are not talking about those being used against——

Mr. TERRELL [continuing]. By ICBM, no.

Mr. PERRY. Yeah. Not United States or United States territories, at least from that delivery system, right? If they chose to package that up, put it on a ship, put it on a plane, somehow deliver it to the West, and use some other methodology—as you know, VX is incredibly pervasive; it only takes a little bit to go a long way—they could use that if they so desired in some kind of attack——

Mr. TERRELL. Yes.

Mr. PERRY [continuing]. In the homeland or somewhere, one of our territories or one of our significant allies, right?

Mr. TERRELL. Correct. Yes.

Mr. PERRY. Okay. Mr. Greene, back to this Lazarus Group. Do you know how they were identified? Do we track them? How do we know—do they identify themselves? Do they claim responsibility for certain things? What is the story on these folks?

Mr. GREENE. So they don't claim responsibility. What we do is we see hundreds of attacks, thousands of attacks every day, and we classify them. We analyze them and are able to compare snippets of code, the techniques, code obfuscation, IP addresses, different techniques. We are able to group certain attacks. So, based on that, the first grouping that I am aware of is 2009; they were reported as being behind some denial-of-service attacks.

So, moving forward from that, what we see is code reuse or other techniques and other tools that are reused that are——

Mr. PERRY. That is how you identify them——

Mr. GREENE. Correct. Yeah.

Mr. PERRY. Do they call themselves the Lazarus Group, or is that our common terminology to describe——

Mr. GREENE. That is our name. There are other names for the same group. But, for us, it is a large group that encompasses virtually all of the activity that has been attributed to North Korea.

Mr. PERRY. Okay. Because you are attributing those actions to different techniques and the markers that you have already discussed, we don't know them by name, individual persons, or locations, or can we glean that at some point from the work that they are doing?

Mr. GREENE. It is getting harder. Oftentimes, you can determine back to a location. We can often find with some high level of confidence a city or even a time zone where something is coming from. But that is through a variety of means. Sometimes we can tell— you know, they leave timestamps when they compile a code. They work 9 to 5. A certain time zone, they take certain holidays off. They have gotten better at hiding that.

What we as a technology company have a hard time doing is saying, who is sitting behind that computer? We may know that they are in a particular, you know, Eastern European country, but what you see is an overlap between sometimes you will have criminals working; sometimes criminals will work for the government; sometimes government workers will moonlight as criminals at night; sometimes you will have these so-called hacktivist groups that will work for the government or be duped into doing it. So we leave that to the intelligence community, that last mile, so to speak, of attribution of the intent. From a technical standpoint, not something we can peer into.

Mr. PERRY. Are these countries typically—these are probably countries—I don't know. Are they typically countries that are not necessarily openly hostile to the United States but not necessarily welcoming as allies in the fight against terrorism or otherwise? Can you characterize that either way?

Mr. GREENE. With the Lazarus Group, I would have to go back. I can get back to you. I am not sure how well we have defined the actual origination point of the attacks or the code. We are grouping them—we are relying, as I said, on the U.S. Government to tell us that this is a North Korean actor. What we can tell with a high level of certainty is that a certain set of attacks are the same. So, for instance, when WannaCry came out, we knew that it was—relatively quickly, had a high level of confidence that this was Lazarus. We didn't know through telemetry that it necessarily came from North Korea. But we knew that this was the same actors for a bunch of different reasons. That became more certain over time. So I don't know—and I could get back to you—that we can tell you specifically—actually, I am quite confident Lazarus—no one really knows who patient one was with the bad outbreak of Lazarus. That hadn't been resolved yet or even what the initial entry point was. But that is one that, as I said, spread autonomously on its own once it got launched.

Mr. PERRY. You are a private entity, and you report your findings and, I imagine, work with the Federal Government and various agencies, whether it is intelligence agencies or otherwise, regarding your findings, but you don't really know whether they go the last mile or not, or do they ever report that to you? Do you ever get any feedback regarding your inputs to know that they were ever resolved? Or how does that work?

Mr. GREENE. Split that in two. With respect to attribution to a nation-state, very rarely I can even think of where we didn't find out by picking up the paper—archaic—looking on-line and seeing that the Government has now attributed X to Y country.

We do get feedback on the quality of the work we do and the assistance we have provided. Again, going back to WannaCry, because it is fresh in my mind, we got a lot of quick feedback from the Government saying, okay, this was helpful, what do you think about that. That was United Kingdom also. We work with other countries as well. So we have a give-and-take on a technical level. But when it comes to—and we were sharing our thoughts on where we thought this was coming from in terms of a connection to Laz-

arus. But we didn't get a, "You are right; we agree with you on
that." We just pass that part along.

Mr. PERRY. You don't know whether Treasury or any other Federal Government agency has pursued these individuals for prosecution or the host countries for notification/apprehension or investigate—you don't know any of that, do you?

Mr. GREENE. Not with Lazarus. I know in other groups they have
indicted Chinese hackers, Iranian hackers, extradited some from—
I believe Ukraine, maybe Bulgaria. We know of some actions, and
we assist in some law enforcement actions. But with respect to
Lazarus, don't know of anything.

Mr. PERRY. Okay. We might ask you to comment further off the
record in an effort to determine what can be done from your viewpoint. It is one thing to identify them. Right? But there is—in my
mind, there is really—I mean, obviously there is a reason to identify them. But if you skip the next series of steps where you go get
them or deter them through the host country that may even not—
they might be victims, as well, right? But if we know and we don't
take the next steps, I mean, that is pretty foolhardy. We have
spent the energy, and the time, and the money, and then we are
moving on to the next threat, right, which is coming momentarily.

Mr. GREENE. From our perspective as a company, looking to protect ourselves, our customers, we are more focused on the how than
the who. The who sometimes informs defense.

There is one thing that you might find interesting: There was a
group of security companies that got together a couple years ago
for something we called Operation Blockbuster, which was a joint
effort to go after Lazarus, to try to degrade their efforts, sharing
a lot of telemetry across different companies. So that is the kind
of thing going to what Mr. Cilluffo was talking about. You see a
lot of security companies. We are competitors, but we also are all
working towards the same end. That was, to some degree, a success. It is the proverbial marathon, not the sprint, though.

Mr. PERRY. Sure. While you might be looking more at methodology than the—the what as opposed to the who—I think the Federal Government has to be looking at both.

Mr. GREENE. Sure.

Mr. PERRY [continuing]. We are glad that you are looking at
the—and your expertise might be in the what. But we have to, I
think, be interested in the who. You can't be, right? You are not
a law enforcement agency——

Mr. GREENE. Right.

Mr. PERRY [continuing]. But the Federal Government is.

Okay. Thank you.

Dr. Pry, why did I write "Louisiana projects" on my notepad?

Mr. PRY. Oh, probably because that is a project that the EMP
Commission launched in cooperation with the Department of
Homeland Security to develop a plan to protect the Louisiana electric grid. We don't know if it is going to survive the death of the
EMP Commission. But, you know, our argument has been that we
don't have to keep studying the problem for years and years, that
we know how to protect the grid now. We can do it now. We can
do it in a cost-effective way.

The people of Louisiana, actually, they are the ones that took the initiative through their Louisiana Public Service Commission to ask Secretary Kelly, who was then the Secretary of Homeland Security, under SEPA, to help them come up with a plan to protect the Louisiana electric grid. DHS is currently doing that. It has already done some good work. But what we want to end up with is a detailed blueprint that they could actually implement, in a cost-effective way, that will to prove to those who disagree with the EMP Commission that we can do the job now, we can do it with the current technology, and it can be done cost-effectively.

Mr. PERRY. We don't have the detailed blueprint at this time?

Mr. PRY. No, not yet. It is just the——

Mr. PERRY. What is it going to take to complete it?

Mr. PRY. It is going to take some time, for one thing. Right now, the people who would normally be working on the plan are helping out in Puerto Rico right now. So that delayed it. Okay? But it will take—once they are over that and they can focus on this plan, it will take 3 to 4 months. They are willing—DHS has been putting $300k into it. It would have been good to have another $170,000. The EMP Commission was going to kick that in, but now we are out of business. So we weren't able to do that. But so for less than—it can probably be done for the $300k.

Mr. PERRY. So you said it is a matter of months, understanding and agreeing that we get past the situation, the disaster, in Puerto Rico, and getting those folks back in power, et cetera. So it is a matter of months there, and less than $200,000 or something like that. Why is the EMP Commission out of business?

Mr. PRY. Well, we were scheduled legislatively—that is a good question and a complicated one. But under our charter—commissions typically last about 18 months. All right? So we reached the end of our life, and nobody asked the Commission to be extended. The Department of Defense didn't. The Department of Homeland Security didn't. You know?

Mr. PERRY. Does that take legislative action, sir, as far as you know? Or is that something that can be done from a regulatory side?

Mr. PRY. It would take legislative action to continue the EMP Commission, or it could be done by a Chairman of a committee. For example, Chairman Johnson, you know, has got the power, as the Chairman of the committee, to basically continue or establish a commission. Now, he wouldn't be able to pay for it on his own. He would have to have the cooperation of the Chairman of the Senate Appropriations Committee if it was to be funded. However, I can tell you the EMP Commissioners have been working for 17 years pro bono. Commissioners do not get paid. I haven't been mostly paid. So we are used to working for nothing.

Mr. PERRY. Okay.

I, like Mr. Higgins, am concerned—I didn't realize Ms. Jackson Lee is here. So I am going to suspend my questions. But I am going to come back to you, Dr. Pry. But I am going to recognize Ms. Jackson Lee for her questions.

Ms. JACKSON LEE. Mr. Chairman, thank you very much. To the witnesses, thank you for yielding to me.

This is a very important discussion. I wish I could spend the time that the Chairman has now spent. But I know that we will have a very extensive record. I appreciate you for that.

Let me just go directly to Mr. Greene and pursue recent reports about North Korea's capacity for attacking the grid. We understand, those of us who have been on this committee—I have chaired the Transportation and Infrastructure Committee. I am on Cybersecurity. So I have seen all of the nuances of homeland security and National security, and we now have a new hurdle. I think one of the most difficult and challenging parts of the hurdle is that 85 percent-plus of our critical infrastructure is in the hands of the private sector. So what capacity does North Korea have in the attack on the critical infrastructure? What would be their inclination? I would suspect that they would say, "Let me drop my other options, and this looks like this is either more fun or more devastating or far-reaching impact," or "I can readily see how the impact is." What is your assessment on that? What is your assessment on our protection against it? What is your assessment on our steps to address something like that?

Mr. GREENE. So I would say the reports that came out in the past week have been about really the first steps of an operation to implicate the grid. The reports that I saw were by the group that we call Lazarus, spear-phishing emails, attempts to get a bridgehead on control systems—I am sorry, just any systems at these energy facilities. Most of the reports have said they have been unsuccessful. But, you know, cyber can be like seeing one bug in your house. Where there is one, there is usually a lot that you can't see. So that suggests to me that there is a lot of other activity going on.

Cyber is one of those things where you really are subject to the weakest-link theory. Eventually, they are going to find a way onto some system. That goes, also, to your question about the preparation of the grid generally. There are a lot of companies that have taken significant steps in recent years. NERC did take a very long time to get some regulations out, but they are being followed. But the problem is you do have the over 3,000 different utilities that Dr. Pry mentioned, and you don't need to compromise the biggest to have some kind of impact.

In terms of whether they are there yet, I haven't seen any evidence to suggest that they have actually gotten onto the control systems. We have seen that with other different actors but not yet with Lazarus. Doesn't mean they are not trying. Now, one thing that may be in our favor is 6,000 sounds like a big number of cyber warriors, so to speak, but it is not as big as some other countries. Control system knowledge, the ability to compromise control systems is fairly specialized. I don't know yea or nay whether they have that, very well could be trying to develop that. But there are a lot of hurdles they have to go through. But, as with the progress we have seen with nuclear and elsewhere, it is not going to stop them from trying. So I hope I answered the breadth of your questions.

Ms. JACKSON LEE. Do you think we are a year away, months away, years away, in terms of their capacity to hack a very, very vital network here in the United States? We are sophisticated. We are dependent on technology. Our power grid is in varying states of repair or disrepair, and our technology is questionable in light of the private-sector ownership as to whether the sufficient firewalls are there. You mentioned the concept of breaching someone's—I call the technological wall and that there is that kind of activity going on.

So where do we need to be in terms of the government? I believe we should not be in a voluntary mode of getting the private sector to be required to document that their systems are secure. We don't have a requirement of secure documentation. To take down our grid is weaponry. So how far away are they from that?

Mr. GREENE. So I don't know the specifics of their capabilities, but I can draw an analogy to this group, Dragonfly Group, extremely sophisticated. We saw them take about 2 years to go from management systems, back-end systems, to control systems. We detected them on those systems earlier this year. So, depending upon their level of expertise, it could take them—it also depends upon, to some degree, on luck, if they find the right vulnerable system and the right human frailty, they could get on sooner. There is a level of understanding that it would take. Just being on the system wouldn't be enough. You have to have a certain level of knowledge of the energy grid generally.

But one thing that we have seen Lazarus to be quite good at is that the reconnaissance element of the operation. So I suspect what we saw reported earlier this week is the proverbial tip of the iceberg of the efforts that have been going on.

Ms. JACKSON LEE. So you believe there is a will and they are making a way, meaning that they would be interested in doing this, this would be one of the elements that they would find attractive in terms of attack on the United States or any other country that they are at odds with?

Mr. GREENE. I think they are not alone in that. There are other major—likely nation-state actors looking to get on the—a beachhead onto the systems. The question becomes, at that point—we talked about it—would be intent and the understanding of the implications of doing it.

With respect to Dragonfly, we have reported that there are no technical limitations left for them to be able to cause impact, significant impact, to energy operators. The bridge they would have to cross is a willingness to do it, understanding the implications to themselves and their own economies and potential retaliation

Ms. JACKSON LEE. Do you think Russia would have any collaboration on this since they were engaged in power attacks in Ukraine?

Mr. GREENE. I just don't have any knowledge on that. I am sorry.

Mr. Chairman, would you yield me a few more minutes? I appreciate it.

Mr. PERRY. Madam.

Ms. JACKSON LEE. Thank you.

I see a head going on Dr. Cilluffo. Do I have it almost right?

Mr. CILLUFFO. Close enough. I have been called much worse.

Ms. JACKSON LEE. It is hard to read it from this distance.

But this is something that I think I am beginning to believe that there are some elements of business choices and the respect we have for the capitalistic system that requires our very keen study. One of them is the infrastructure of cyber that is in the private sector and what firewalls that have an overwhelming impact. So I yield to you, and I want to go to Mr. Terrell. So I don't want to lose my—on another matter, Mr. Terrell.

Yes.

Mr. CILLUFFO. Ms. Jackson Lee, I mean, thank you for the question. I think you raise an important point here. First, not all critical infrastructure is equally critical. When you get to the most critical, those that affect our so-called lifeline sectors, that affect public safety, National security, and economic security, the grid is at the top of the list. I don't care how robust everything else is, if you don't have power, it is kind of futile.

Ms. JACKSON LEE. There you are.

Mr. CILLUFFO. So, yes, they are a unique set of entities.

On the Russia side, what they demonstrated both in 2015 and 2016, a Rubicon was crossed in that case. So we all thought, coulda, shoulda, woulda, that these were potential threats. But in this case, they actually intended to signal a capability. Because they followed up the disruptive attacks with a digital telephony denial-of-service attack, basically an in-your-face "ha ha, we got ya" response to the first attack.

The reason I jumped into this fray was because, obviously, North Korea is dependent upon China for much of its support and the like. But you are slowly starting to see Russia fill that breach. In fact, it was a Russian company that just moved in to provide internet access service to North Korea—since the Chinese capabilities have been minimized—to have back-end capability. So I do think you have got a bigger set of issues here. There is quite a bit of chatter that Russia has been supporting and working—whether the State, or whether through its proxies, organized crime, hard to discern who is behind that clickety-clack of the keyboard. But there is a lot of interest there.

This comes to a point, Mr. Chairman, you brought up earlier. One of the most vexing challenges is that you are—there are digital safe havens. A vast majority of these bad actors are playing in China and Russia. We lack extradition treaties with both of those countries. The reality is, is we have to get more and more creative to be able to extradite them when they go to countries that the United States does have a cooperative relationship.

So this issue, as complex it is vis-á-vis North Korea, the cyber issue also has to be seen—it can't be seen in isolation of all of these other matters, because it really is about the safe havens. Russia and China are there, and I think Russia is filling the breach that China has been abrogating in North Korea.

Ms. JACKSON LEE. He is giving me—I am not going to look in his direction because his gavel might be moving. So I am going to take his kindness. I am very glad he had this hearing.

I think you should give us, maybe in writing, our marching orders. Don't think that I am asking you to be presumptuous. So you said safe havens. I would like to get maybe five points for the record. If you have five points that you can say quickly without explanation, the safe havens. You know, I am concerned about the vastness of the private sector in these critical areas that you have talked about. The firewall that we have, you know, it is in the private sector. We have voluntary—and if you call us, we can come. What more can we do that strengthens their protection, if, in fact, their own internal systems are not where they need to be? Because this is National security issues when another country hacks XYZ Corporation that is dealing with the power grid or dealing with the hospitals or dealing with research. It is very important.

Mr. CILLUFFO. Is that a QFR? Is that question for me to follow up on? Or are you looking for?

Ms. JACKSON LEE. Well, give me one because I am going to go to Professor——

Mr. CILLUFFO. Well, I—so this is not to the punt the issue——

Ms. JACKSON LEE. Give me——

Mr. CILLUFFO [continuing]. But, quite honestly, I don't think we are ever going to firewall our way out of this problem. By that I mean the initiative remains with the attacker. So, if you think of it in the traditional red-blue military kind of environment, we have to shape the environment so it is in our best interest to—so that is not to abrogate all the cybersecurity responsibilities, but the initiative will always be with the attacker. The attack surface is growing exponentially. Every day, the attack surface grows, and security still tends to be an afterthought. When we start thinking of the internet of things and the network devices that are coming on board, we are never going to simply be able to firewall our way out of this problem.

I actually feel the private sector has been given an unfair—they are defending against nation-states. So we have to level that playing field. Without going into a totally different direction, I think we need to be a little more proactive in shaping the environment so it is in our best interests.

Ms. JACKSON LEE. Thank you. This needs to be pursued along other lines. I have probably a different view. But let me just—but I thank you for that view. The safe havens is something that we need to ascertain.

Mr. Terrell, I want to get to the question of North Korea's danger to the homeland. Maybe get you to—first of all, let me say that I am a proponent of the non-nuclear agreement with Iran. You might offer to comment on the idea of—first of all, that doesn't mean that you do not look at the compliance and other elements that may need to be of concern. That is not a blanket. That is a vigilant on the other elements of Iran's terrorism, propping up Assad, and other things. But when you look to the agreement, you have to look to the four corners of it, whether or not there is compliance, whether there is access. All of those, at this point, have not been negated.

But I think the point that I want to raise is, if you can ascertain—if you said it, please forgive me, but I would like to hear it—where North Korea is right now in their capacity. I don't want the news articles, they can get to Alaska, they can get here, wherever their head of government chooses to say on any given day. But your ascertaining his—where he is, where the country is, and the likelihood of his efforts, if you will, that would be helpful.

Mr. TERRELL. Yes, ma'am. You know, with respect to the difference between Iran and North Korea, just very quickly, we have to deal with every country and every threat in the unique situation that that threat exists in. So, you know, Iran doesn't match perfectly to North Korea. North Korea doesn't match perfectly to Russia. So, you know, approaching each one tailored to that threat is important.

So where North Korea sits with their willingness and ability to attack the homeland today using nuclear or chemical weapons, you know, the nuclear program, he has an ability to employ nuclear weapons today. It is a matter of where can he employ them and when and why would he employ them. So, in understanding North Korean rationale, they are an extremely rational actor from their perspective. They do things that are in their national interests, in solidifying his security as the head of state, in solidifying his security within the region.

This is—he has a population surrounding him that almost nobody remembers a time when the Kim family was not in charge. For 67 years, they have all been told everything that is wrong in North Korea is the Americans' fault.

Ms. JACKSON LEE. Uh-huh.

Mr. TERRELL. So, when pushed into a corner, he will have reason, from his perspective, he can create a rationality to attack, if he feels he needs to. He is going to try to deter us because he still has two operational regional objectives to try to accomplish. The family has always said unification of the Korean Peninsula is important. So can he do that in such a way where he can keep the United States from not supporting the Republic of Korea and not supporting Japan and keep Japan out of a war? Can he do this either—or, if he can't reunify initially, can he reach an actual peace treaty on the peninsula that solidifies his position? Because in solidifying his position with just a peace treaty, he can say, "I have finished what my grandfather started," and he sets himself up for long-term control in North Korea, which is why the—a global campaign pressure or pressure campaign that cuts off funding from the outside, cuts out support, weakens that position.

So the challenge becomes, you know, can he attack us? Yes. Can he attack us effectively yet? He is almost there.

The North Koreans have also demonstrated they are not nearly as interested in the actual precision that we may be interested in. If he can attack Seattle, does he care if he can attack directly at and hit directly on top of the Space Needle? No. But if he can hit Seattle, he can hit Seattle. If he can hit the United States, he can hit the United States. So his threshold of use may be lower than ours. His threshold of accuracy will be lower than ours.

So, you know, we may not be there tonight. We may be there next week, or we may be there next month. But we are at the point where he is going to have the ability to attack the United States and with an intent of killing Americans. You know, just hurting us a little bit isn't as important to him as it is killing us. In North Korea, they remember the U.S. bombing campaign during the Korean war was, if there is two bricks stacked on top of each other, the United States is going to destroy those two bricks. They are going to want to inflict as much damage as they possibly can if they attack.

Mr. PERRY. Will the gentlelady yield? I have got a hard stop.

Ms. JACKSON LEE. I would be happy to yield. Mr. Chairman, is he allowed to say his one action to stop that? I will be happy to yield back, Mr. Chairman.

What is our action? What is our action? I believe if he sees other agreements being abandoned, we certainly don't have an opportunity of diplomacy. But go right ahead.

Mr. TERRELL. The overall means of dealing with North Korea today, we are at this point where we have to continue the campaign pressure or the pressure campaign. We have to demonstrate our resolve. We have to be able to talk to them.

It may not actually end up being a negotiated solution. But over, you know, the entire course of the Cold War, in deterrence with Russia, we talked to the Russians. We talked to the Soviets. They understood our message. We understood their message.

We have to have those means of being able to talk to the North Koreans so we can have an effective deterrent while we get to a solution that hopefully does not include going to war.

Mr. PERRY. The Chair thanks the gentleman.

The Chair thanks the gentlelady.

Ms. JACKSON LEE. Mr. Chairman, you have been generous with your time. Thank you.

Mr. PERRY. Dr. Pry, I just want to finish up here with you, if I could. I, too, like Mr. Higgins, am concerned and interested in the satellite array and the capabilities therewith that North Korea has. Can they potentially launch on EMP device from one of those satellites? Is it something that is launched from the satellite? Does the satellite come out of orbit? Does the satellite deploy something? How does that work?

Mr. PRY. We are concerned because the satellites, the orbit, the trajectory, the purpose of this, resembles this secret weapon the Soviets came up with during the Cold War called the Fractional Orbital Bombardment System. Basically, the satellite has a nuclear weapon inside of it. You orbit the satellite so it is at the optimum altitude already for putting an EMP field——

Mr. PERRY. You are saying it is currently there right now?

Mr. PRY. Yeah, it is. It passes over us several times a day at that place. All you have to do is detonate it when it arrives. Because we don't have ballistic missile early warning radars facing south, we don't have interceptors facing south, we are blind, defenseless from that direction, which is why it is on a south polar orbit.

Now they have got two of them there. I find it—we might have actually seen a dry run of a North Korean total information warfare operation back during the 2013 nuclear crisis we had with North Korea after their third nuclear test. That was on April 16, 2013. You know, it coincided with lots of cyber activity attacks from North Korea. But that was the day of the Metcalf transformer shooting. Okay? We don't know who did that. But when the people that train the U.S. Navy SEALs went in there, they said they thought this was a nation-state operation. This was done the way the SEALs would have done it in terms of all their techniques. On that very day is the day the KMS–2 passed over Washington, DC, and New York City. So you had events that threatened the western grid and the eastern grid simultaneously on that day. We don't know if it was North Korea that did Metcalf. But for sure that was their satellite passing over Washington, DC, and the New York City corridor.

Mr. PERRY. So the two satellites they have right now, they—apparently, one at least passes over New York City—the East Coast, New York City, Washington, DC, and the other one?

Mr. PRY. Well, they actually—every time they do an orbit, they pass other another 90 miles to the east. So there are times——

Mr. PERRY. I see.

Mr. PRY [continuing]. When it is right over the center of the United States and then passes over the eastern——

Mr. PERRY. And there are times, apparently, that there are none or potentially none——

Mr. PRY. Yes. That is——

Mr. PERRY [continuing]. Over the United States? But your testimony indicates that they would like to fill the array so that there is ever one present?

Mr. PRY. Right. I mean, it used to be that, basically, you would have to wait 90 minutes. All right? Now, it is 45 minutes.

Mr. PERRY. We don't know what is in the satellite?

Mr. PRY. No, we don't. According to the North Koreans' official position, it is an Earth observation satellite for peaceful purposes. But then Kim Jong-un and North Korean press have actually included it in their descriptions as part of their nuclear deterrent. There are quotations from them to that effect in the——

Mr. PERRY. When you say a deterrent, they might say: Well, look, we are just photographing sites where nuclear armaments in the United States might be launched from to see if there is any activity, and, thus, it is a deterrent.

I mean, right? They could say that.

Mr. PRY. Of course, they could say that. They have also described it as a peaceful, you know, satellite. But why they would be interested in, I mean, the health of the forests in North America is, you know, open to question.

Mr. PERRY. Right. I suspect they would consider disruption, removal, whatever you want to call it, of that satellite or any of those satellites as an act of aggression and war.

Mr. PRY. Sure. But the satellites are illegal in the first place. They were not supposed to have been launching satellites, which is part—and not on that trajectory.

Mr. PERRY. So what is the recourse for nation-states or nations that launch satellites in violation of whatever sanction or whatever U.N. requirements, whatever requirements are that make them illegal? What is the remedy?

Mr. PRY. I think the only remedy for that is going to be to shoot those satellites down.

Mr. PERRY. Why hasn't that been done already?

Mr. PRY. I don't know. I don't know why it hasn't been done.

Mr. PERRY. Gentlemen, you have been very gracious with your time. We appreciate your testimony more than you can imagine. We appreciate your diligence in being here and waiting the extra time for the vote and then staying after. We probably will have some due-outs for at least some of you, I know I will, and maybe we will see you again. We hope we have better news or at least improved news the next time we get together.

At this time, the Chair thanks the witnesses for their valuable testimony and the Members for their questions. Members may have some additional questions for the witnesses, and we will ask you to respond to these in writing.

Pursuant to committee rule VII(D), the hearing record will remain open for 10 days.

Without objection, the subcommittee stands adjourned.

[Whereupon, at 4:48 p.m., the subcommittee was adjourned.]

APPENDIX

QUESTIONS FROM CHAIRMAN SCOTT PERRY FOR FRANK J. CILLUFFO

Question 1a. As the owners and operators of critical infrastructure, the private sector is placed in a unique position to maintain and operate their business while at the same time trying to defend themselves against potential, unwanted attacks from foreign militaries or foreign intelligence services.

What type of public-private partnerships can be put in place to assist private industry, who you labeled as "on the front lines of this battle," in thwarting attacks?

Answer. Response was not received at the time of publication.

Question 1b. Additionally, during the hearing, you mentioned setting up a "tiger team" to specifically deal with the North Korean threat. Can you elaborate on this point? Who would comprise this team and what agency would lead this effort?

Answer. Response was not received at the time of publication.

QUESTIONS FROM HONORABLE JOHN RATCLIFFE FOR FRANK J. CILLUFFO

Question 1. Some nations outsource their malicious cyber work. They hire hackers using covert means or otherwise distance themselves from the actual hack. These "hackers-for-hire" make attributing attacks to particular nations difficult. Do the North Korean's use similar tactics when conducting their cyber campaigns or are they more overt in their tactics?

Answer. Response was not received at the time of publication.

Question 2. What are the kinds of things experts look for when attributing particular cyber attacks to North Korea? Does their cyber activity have unique characteristics—technical or otherwise?

Answer. Response was not received at the time of publication.

Question 3. What can we do to deter North Korean cyber actors?

Answer. Response was not received at the time of publication.

QUESTIONS FROM CHAIRMAN SCOTT PERRY FOR JEFF GREENE

Question 1a. During the hearing, you discussed the coordinated response to the Wannacry ransomware attack which occurred in May 2017. You stated: "The Wannacry response was probably the best public-private partnership I have ever seen." However, you also stated that you remain concerned that a response of that type was somewhat relationship-based and needs to be more structured.

What type of formalized process of information sharing between government and industry to you suggest?

Answer. Response was not received at the time of publication.

Question 1b. Which Government agency should lead this effort?

Answer. Response was not received at the time of publication.

QUESTIONS FROM HONORABLE JOHN RATCLIFFE FOR JEFF GREENE

Question 1. Some nations outsource their malicious cyber work. They hire hackers using covert means or otherwise distance themselves from the actual hack. These "hackers-for-hire" make attributing attacks to particular nations difficult. Do the North Koreans use similar tactics when conducting their cyber campaigns or are they more overt in their tactics?

Answer. Response was not received at the time of publication.

Question 2. What are the kinds of things experts look for when attributing particular cyber attacks to North Korea? Does their cyber activity have unique characteristics—technical or otherwise?

Answer. Response was not received at the time of publication.

Question 3. What can we do to deter North Korean cyber actors?

Answer. Response was not received at the time of publication.

66

Question 1. If an EMP attack were to occur, what electronic components or systems would sustain the most damage? Do you know if any attempt has been made to protect these systems?

Answer. All electronic components and systems would be at risk in an EMP attack. Long-line and large systems and their electronic components—for example, the 99 operating U.S. nuclear power reactors and their on-site stored spent fuel cooling systems, power grids, telecommunications, pipelines (gas, oil, chemical, water etc.)—would be most at risk because they would collect and could be damaged by both high-frequency (E1) and low-frequency (E3) EMP. Supervisory Control And Data Acquisition Systems (SCADAS) are among the most vulnerable and most important electronic systems. SCADAS numbering in the millions make possible our modern electronic society, running everything from electric grids to traffic lights. While there are some cases where utilities and industry have voluntarily protected some of their SCADAS and other critical electronics from EMP, on the whole the critical National infrastructures are unprotected.

Question 2. The Congressional EMP Commission recently terminated. How do you think this will impact the Department of Homeland Security as they move forward in EMP preparedness, especially in light of North Korea?

Answer. Termination of the EMP Commission will halt and reverse progress being made toward National EMP preparedness, despite the clear and present danger of an EMP attack from North Korea. For example, the Louisiana Project, started and supported by the EMP Commission, is likely to be killed by DHS, now that the EMP Commission is terminated. In this project DHS is working with the Louisiana Public Service Commission to develop a plan to protect the Louisiana electric grid—to prove that cost-effective EMP protection can be accomplished now, pioneering a pathway toward EMP preparedness for all the States. The Louisiana Project is justified by and is an example of implementation of the Critical Infrastructure Protection Act (CIPA). Yet the recently established DHS EMP Task Force, that owes a report to Congress in December on CIPA implementation, was not even aware of the Louisiana Project, and showed no interest in the Louisiana Project. Obama-holdovers and bureaucrats at DHS who have most obstructed progress toward National EMP preparedness have been promoted by the current administration, while those most committed to EMP preparedness are an endangered species. DHS and DOE are still following the Obama administration's policy on EMP—let the North American Electric Reliability Corporation (NERC) and the electric power industry drive the bus. Let the National labs takeover the EMP problem to be used as a cash cow to milk for millions of dollars in unnecessary and erroneous studies, that will justify NERC inaction on EMP.

Question 3. Why would North Korea strike the United States with an EMP attack instead of a more traditional bomb, if they have the capabilities for both?

Answer. A traditional bomb can be used to make an EMP attack or blast a city, and North Korea might well do both. Indeed, in order to blast U.S. cities, North Korea would have to penetrate U.S. National Missile Defenses, which could be facilitated by a precursor nuclear EMP attack. North Korea might also salvage-fuse warheads aimed at U.S. cities so that, if they are intercepted, they detonate for EMP attack. Compared to traditional use of a nuclear weapon for blasting a city, nuclear EMP attack is easier to execute and would be more effective at damaging the Nation's life-sustaining critical infrastructures and capabilities Nation-wide that are essential for military power projection. Unlike blasting a city, EMP attack does not require a reentry vehicle to penetrate the atmosphere or an accurate guidance system. Unlike blasting a city, a single nuclear weapon used for EMP can attack the whole Nation.

○